THE
FINANCIAL
RECOVERY
WORKBOOK

THE
FINANCIAL
RECOVERY
WORKBOOK

A STEP-BY-STEP PLAN FOR

REGAINING CONTROL OF YOUR MONEY

AND YOUR LIFE DURING AND AFTER

A PERSONAL FINANCIAL CRISIS

MICHELE CAGAN, CPA
Author of *Investing 101*

ADAMS MEDIA

NEW YORK LONDON TORONTO SYDNEY NEW DELHI

Aadamsmedia

Adams Media
An Imprint of Simon & Schuster, Inc.
100 Technology Center Drive
Stoughton, Massachusetts 02072

First Adams Media trade paperback edition July 2021

ADAMS MEDIA and colophon are trademarks of Simon & Schuster.

For information about special discounts for bulk purchases, please contact Simon & Schuster Special Sales at 1-866-506-1949 or business@simonandschuster.com.

The Simon & Schuster Speakers Bureau can bring authors to your live event. For more information or to book an event contact the Simon & Schuster Speakers Bureau at 1-866-248-3049 or visit our website at www.simonspeakers.com.

Interior design by Colleen Cunningham and Julia Jacintho
Interior images © Getty Images/-VICTOR-

Manufactured in the United States of America

1 2021

ISBN 978-1-5072-1641-5

DEDICATION

Thanks, Jenny, for helping me
through the hardest times.

CONTENTS

INTRODUCTION

Need help figuring out how to afford unplanned expenses? Wondering whether to max out credit cards, raid your 401(k), or take out a personal loan? When you're stuck in a financial hole, it can feel impossible to find your way out. Plus, you're dealing with whatever landed you in that situation—health crisis, divorce, job loss—at the same time you have to handle the financial fallout. But believe it or not, the money piece can be the easiest thing to control, even when everything else feels completely overwhelming. And while it takes time to dig out and rebuild, you can do it—one step at a time.

The Financial Recovery Workbook grew out of my personal experience and expertise working with clients for more than twenty years. This workbook will walk you through overcoming your financial setbacks, no matter what caused them, so you can move into a more secure future. Inside you'll find specific steps and detailed worksheets that target different pieces of your financial healing, build up safety nets, and plan for prosperity (downloadable Excel spreadsheets for each worksheet can be found at https://michelecagancpa.com/FinRec101 with the password F1n@nc!@LRecOvery!). As you move through the chapters that follow, you'll:

- Take a Financial Fears Inventory to sort the facts from the emotions of your situation
- Get a true picture of how much you owe by making a debt table

- Refocus your goals and create a money management plan to help you achieve them
- Take stock of the talents you have that can help bring in more money to cover unexpected costs
- Create a calendar for paying bills to make sure you're never late with a payment
- Monitor your finances regularly to track your progress and strengthen your position
- Discover additional tools and resources for continued financial success

No matter what caused your money troubles, you can get through them. With every positive action that you take, you'll move closer to recovery and security. And along the way, you'll learn critical skills that can help you weather any future financial storm with confidence.

CHAPTER ONE

FACING THE FEARS AND FINDING THE FACTS

You've been hit by a crisis that put you in a difficult financial position, and you may be afraid that you'll never be able to get back to a secure place or make future financial progress. That fear can be overwhelming, and it may lead to other negative emotions like guilt, shame, and self-doubt.

The only way to fight those fears is to name them and face them, and in the following chapter, you'll do just that. You'll use the Financial Fears Inventory worksheet to identify the fears that may be sabotaging you. Once you've named those fears, you can begin to defuse them and move forward from them. You'll also discover some of the financial circumstances that are unique to your crisis, along with targeted tips to help you work through them. Because even though some financial issues (like running through savings or increasing debt) will be the same for most types of crises, managing the fallout from a natural disaster is much different than handling a health crisis or a divorce, for example. Facing your financial situation can be tough, and that may make you want to avoid taking a close look. But gathering your financial facts will simplify your situation and give you a sense of direction. In fact, you may find out that you're in better financial shape than you thought and that you have access to resources you didn't realize you could use.

Accept That Emergencies and Major Life Changes Affect Finances

A lot of situations can take a temporary toll on your finances, and most of us have to deal with one or more of these at some point in life. Along with all of your regular expenses, your crisis will create its own extra costs and consume resources you were counting on to cover other things. The key to getting through a crisis and coming out in a place of financial security involves identifying and planning for the specific issues you may face within your own situation.

Some of the moves you'll make throughout this workbook to protect your current and future finances will be the same regardless of which crisis you're dealing with. Others will be targeted more toward the specific situation. And all of those moves will come together in your unique financial recovery plan. In the following sections, you'll get a close-up view of the common crises people face, and the financial issues they can cause.

HEALTH CRISIS

We usually don't expect health emergencies, but they have to be dealt with no matter how they'll affect your finances. When you're dealing with broken bones, a cancer diagnoses, or mental health struggles for example, you can't skimp on care. Health situations add an extra level of financial frustration because it can be difficult (sometimes impossible) to know how much they'll cost you until after the fact. Plus, on top of the immediate emergency costs, you may be facing long-term ongoing expenses that will force you to revisit your monthly budget. You'll have to coordinate insurance, submit claims, and possibly negotiate with care providers to stay on top of those expenses.

Take It from a CPA

When my son was admitted to the hospital, I tried to find out my approximate share of costs ahead of time, but no one could (or would) tell me. Not the insurance company, not the hospital, not the benefits coordinator. I had no idea whether his hospital stay would cost me $2,000 or $10,000 or $30,000...or more. That made it difficult to budget for, which made me super-anxious and kept me up a lot of nights.

I immediately created my crisis budget, including guesses of what those bills would look like. As they started to trickle in, I realized that I'd been way off about my share of costs. Another round of financial anxiety started to strike, and I knew a revised plan was the only way to calm things down. So I focused on getting all of my facts together and creating my plan to deal with these bills. And in this book I'll share my process with you, and walk you through the steps I took to come out financially secure and confident on the other side.

Then there's the other side of this crisis: time. When you've experienced a health crisis, you may be unable to work. When someone you love is suffering, you may have to devote a lot of your time to caretaking. Either way, it can limit the time and energy you'd normally be able to devote to solving problems and bringing in money. That's why it's important to create a plan with manageable steps to deal with the financial piece.

DIVORCE

Sometimes a person knows a divorce is coming, and other times they are blindsided by it. In either case, going through a divorce can drain your finances unless you take proactive steps to avoid that. Even in the best of circumstances, both partners typically face immediate financial setbacks and higher expenses. Your income-to-expense ratio will change dramatically, with expenses eating up a larger portion of the money you have coming in. Maintaining two households costs a lot more than supporting one, especially in the beginning when you may have to replace dozens of household items and pay your lawyer.

Keep an Eagle Eye on Legal Bills

Legal fees rank among the biggest financial problems for people going through divorce. That's not surprising: As of 2019 the average divorce costs $12,900, according to Martindale-Nolo Research. And depending on your situation, your costs could be double—even triple—that. Pay attention to when and how often you're turning to your legal team. Try to limit communications to purely legal matters, rather than financial or emotional issues.

Mapping out a plan to cover all of these new costs will help you:

- Move forward with your finances
- Create your new home
- Reduce at least some of your stress
- Avoid drowning in new debt
- Build a more secure and prosperous financial future

Starting over on your own calls for some big adjustments in your life. Creating a plan to tackle the money-related changes can reduce fear and uncertainty. Plus, it will help you avoid the risk of a bigger financial crisis, and increase your financial confidence and security.

DEATH

When you lose someone important in your life, finances may be the last thing you want to deal with. But during this time, a lot of money-related issues will need to be untangled, and that includes figuring out how to cope financially. Your financial situation will depend partly on whether you receive life insurance proceeds or other death benefits, but those can take time—and you'll still need to take care of pressing needs right away. Getting all of your financial information organized will remove a layer of worry from your situation. While a lot of other areas of your life may feel out of control, the financial recovery moves in this workbook will help you gain control of that piece.

Take Time with Tasks

After the death of a spouse or partner, you'll be faced with dozens of decisions, but you don't have to deal with all of them at once. Split them into a few buckets: one for immediately necessary tasks, one for things that need to be done soon but not right away (within three to twelve months), and one for things that can wait until next year.

Organizing your finances after a death can be especially tricky if you lost a partner who took care of the lion's share of them. You may have a limited picture of where your money is or the amount of outstanding debt. It may be difficult—at least at first—to access all of the accounts, especially if your name wasn't originally on them. You may not know which bills are on autopay and which need immediate attention. But you can manage all of these financial unknowns, one at a time, by creating a thoughtful plan and laying out clear steps to deal with each piece.

JOB LOSS

Losing a job—especially if you're the primary earner in your household—can cause a sudden financial shock. On top of that, job loss often comes with emotional fallout, which can make it harder to focus on the immediate financial issues at the same time that you're trying to find a new job. Applying for unemployment and other social benefits may feel uncomfortable—like you're admitting defeat—but they're there exactly for this situation. These safety nets offer a bridge between jobs, and it's important for your financial stability to take advantage of everything that can help you meet your budget necessities. Remember: It's unemployment *insurance*. No different than being in a car accident and getting a check from the insurance company to fix your car.

Showcase Yourself to Find a New Job

Two of the most important tools you'll want for your job search are a customized resume and a strong, current *LinkedIn* profile to match. You want to stand out, which can be especially hard when applying for jobs online, so make sure your resume shines. Highlight your biggest accomplishments and strongest skills rather than focusing on job responsibilities. Use specific keywords tailored to the jobs you want, to ensure you'll pop up when recruiters search for candidates.

Losing your job may also mean losing your employer-related insurance: health, life, and disability. To get all of that coverage back on track can call for a cash outlay you weren't expecting to deal with, so start with health insurance and work from there. Losing coverage combined with the sudden loss of a steady paycheck can put your finances in a precarious position. That's a lot to overcome, but you *can* push through and end up with a better job and in a more secure financial situation than ever before.

MARKET CRASH CLOSE TO OR AFTER RETIREMENT

It's hard to watch your portfolio lose value at any time, but when you're about to retire or are retired already, the financial shock of a market crash can lead to all-out panic. Your instinct will tell you to sell every stock and stock fund in your portfolio. That can lead to impulsive choices that end up making your future financial situation even worse. Before you sell a single investment, stop and make a plan. Selling without a well-thought-out plan only locks in your losses, and right now they're still just on paper.

You can weather a market downturn by making careful moves—and those don't involve panic selling. Instead, you'll want to focus on your immediate financial needs and give the bulk of your portfolio an opportunity to rebound (and with time, it will). By following the steps toward financial recovery laid out in this book, you'll be able to cover your current needs with minimal damage to your nest egg. After all, you want that money to last for a very long time.

NATURAL DISASTER

From hurricanes to wildfires to earthquakes, natural disasters seem to be coming harder and faster every year. Any of these can leave you with substantial damage to your home and/or belongings, so you have to replace things. In most cases, some kind of insurance will cover at least a portion of your losses, but you'll still have to manage your deductible. Plus, it can take months (at least) to get insurance checks, leaving you with a money gap that needs to be filled right away.

Being forced out of your home can lead to other financial dilemmas too. For example, you may not be able to get mail from government agencies or from utility, insurance, or mortgage companies, so you might be unable to respond to notices on time. Or you may still be responsible for making car payments even if your car was totaled in the disaster. You may have lost credit and debit cards, and even your identification, which can make it hard to access your accounts.

These are just some of the finance-related issues you may face during a natural disaster—but luckily there is a lot of help available. Tap in to every local, state, and federal government resource you can access, including direct financial aid and low-interest loans. Contact your bank as soon as possible to find out how you can quickly regain access to your money. And as soon as you can manage it, start putting together your financial recovery plan so you can move quickly through this crisis and rebuild your life.

Understand the Financial Fallout from a Crisis

No matter what kind of crisis situation you're dealing with, it will affect your finances, sometimes in ways that you don't expect. My grandmother always said that "everything costs more and takes longer than you expect," and that's especially true during a crisis. When you're faced with an emergency, you won't necessarily have time to shop around for the most cost-effective solutions, so you may end up paying more than you otherwise would have. That's part of the territory when it comes to emergencies, so don't be hard on yourself if you feel like you've overpaid for something.

As you've learned previously in this chapter, financial fallout can include a wide range of issues, and those may be different depending on your specific crisis and existing financial situation. Generally, though, you'll face some common problems, no matter what has occurred. These include:

- Extra expenses generated by the emergency
- Burning through emergency savings
- Increased use of credit cards to cover regular expenses
- Needing to prioritize expenses and choosing which will get paid
- Scrambling to find ways to bring money in
- Needing to downsize expenses, sometimes to an uncomfortable level
- Dealing with insurance companies and government agencies for assistance
- Being unable to pay all of your bills
- Watching your credit score drop
- Falling behind on debt repayment
- Raiding retirement accounts

That may sound overwhelming, but remember that it's temporary. Your emergency will have an endpoint, and so will the financial fallout. You will get your finances back on track with time and a strong plan. You'll rebuild savings and watch them grow. You'll pay off your debt, which will free up more money to put toward your savings goals and wealth-building efforts.

When you're stuck in the middle of all of this, it can be hard to see the other side—but it's there and you will reach it. That's why this workbook contains all of the steps you need to take to enjoy a full financial recovery. And if you keep working your plan and following the steps you've set out for yourself, you will get there.

Recognize Your Financial Fears

Fear can keep you stuck in a bad situation. It can lead you into panic-based decisions that seem right in the moment but end up harming your finances. Other times it can paralyze your decision-making and keep you from taking the necessary steps to reclaim control of your situation. But you can conquer that fear and make progress in a positive direction.

The best way to overcome your financial fears is to recognize and accept them. Your feelings are valid, and ignoring or judging them can interfere with your financial recovery. So take a moment to think about your feelings, especially the ones that are so powerful they can affect your actions.

Common financial fears (and I've experienced many of these myself) include being afraid that:

- You'll lose everything
- You'll lose your home/end up homeless
- You won't be able to manage
- You'll let your family (and yourself) down
- You'll make the situation worse
- You'll go bankrupt
- You won't ever be able to retire/stop working

You may recognize some of the financial fears listed here, or yours may be totally different. No matter what your financial fears look like, they can trigger your body's stress hormones and send your emotions into overdrive. Taking the time to list the things that frighten you can help you move past them. The Financial Fears Inventory worksheet at the end of this chapter can help you sort through any fears that could be making it harder for you to keep moving forward. It's the first step toward transforming your fears into positive actions that will help land you in a place of true financial security.

THE EMOTIONS OF FINANCIAL HARDSHIP

When you're facing financial hardship, a lot of other negative emotions can come up along with fear. You may be feeling guilt or shame and blame yourself for "being in this mess." You may feel defeated or deflated, like you're not good enough or this wouldn't have happened (this is especially common with job loss and divorce).

It's tough to not get stuck in these feelings, but they won't serve you in your quest for financial recovery. They keep you bogged down in the past and the events that brought you to where you are right now. Be as kind to yourself as you can, and make sure to acknowledge the positive steps you're taking. Give yourself credit for the things you're doing right—and you are doing a lot of things right.

Remember, feelings aren't facts, and separating the two can help you move forward. Take some time to fill out the Separate Feelings, Thoughts, Facts, and Actions worksheet at the end of this chapter. It can help you get a clearer picture of the facts "on the ground" (as my dad used to say). You may be surprised by some of the things your emotional brain has been telling you. Once you've identified your fears, sorted out your feelings and thoughts, and looked at some concrete facts, it will be easier to start moving forward.

Take It from a CPA

Divorce and a job loss—at the same time—made me feel like a failure as a person and as a mother. Guilt and self-blame hit me hard, and I started to spin out about the possibility of never finding another job, having our power turned off, my kid struggling, losing our home, and a thousand other upsetting scenarios. To break myself out of that spiral, my therapist suggested I write down those negative messages in a journal. Seeing them on paper helped me get a handle on what I was *really* facing, versus what I was afraid of facing, and figure out next steps.

However you ended up in this crisis situation, it's already happened. Blaming and judging yourself for the past can interfere with making plans to fix your financial future. What's most important is what happens next—and that's something you *can* control.

Face and Accept Your Situation to Change It

The only way to get through your financial crisis is to face it head-on. You can't begin to repair your finances until you've acknowledged and accepted the situation you're in. I know that's hard to do—in a weird way, accepting that things are this bad can feel like accepting failure. But it's actually the opposite. Looking squarely at your finances counts as a success. Every step—no matter how small—you take to fix the situation is another win. And when you follow the path in this workbook, your wins will start adding up and piling on.

You've already taken some positive, proactive steps. You're reading this book, and you've started on the path to financial recovery by starting the worksheets. As you gather, organize, and analyze your financial situation, you'll begin to come to terms with it. Then you can start making realistic plans to manage the situation in the way that's the least harmful to your long-term financial health. Even things that don't seem like victories are. For example, not touching your savings for a week counts as a win. So does boosting the cash coming in, cutting a single expense, or using credit card points instead of cash to buy household supplies. All of these help protect your current and future financial situation— and all of them are solid victories.

You're Not in This Alone

Managing a life crisis and financial problems at the same time can leave you completely drained. And while your instinct may be to isolate yourself, staying connected can help keep you from drowning in stress. And you may be surprised at the different ways people in your circle can help you. If they want to lend a hand—watch your kids for an afternoon, do your grocery shopping, etc.—let them.

You can change your financial picture for the better. It may take some time, effort, and sacrifice right now. You'll need to take a much more active role in managing your money every day and pay closer attention than you're probably used to doing. That's how your situation will begin to improve, day by day. And even if you experience some additional setbacks, you'll have the skills, resources, and confidence to overcome them. You can weather this financial crisis and set yourself and your family up for a more secure financial future. You've got this.

Chapter Worksheets

The following worksheets will help you fully focus and begin working through your current money issues. Don't worry about filling these in perfectly—everyone has their own way of completing them. It's also a good idea to revisit them as you're moving through your crisis. Visit https://michelecagancpa.com/FinRec101 for downloadable versions (password: F1n@nc!@LRec0very!).

FINANCIAL FEARS INVENTORY

✅ This worksheet can help you identify the fears you have surrounding your financial struggle. Don't filter yourself here: Being honest about your fears is the first step toward conquering them. Use the examples to guide you. Naming these emotions helps you confront them, and reframe them in ways that will be more constructive for you. As you name each fear, think about what steps you might take if it did happen.

Financial Fear Examples:

- **I'm afraid that I'll make the wrong money move.**
   If that happens, I will figure out how to fix it and I'll know how to handle it in the future.

- **I'm afraid that I'll make things worse.**
   If that happens, I can talk to a financial coach or other professional to help me get on the right track.

- **I'm afraid of disappointing my family.**
   I can talk to my family about the situation and their expectations, and include them as I move through the steps of financial recovery.

- **I'm afraid of losing my home.**
   There are steps I can take to prevent that, but if it happens, I will find a new place to live.

My Financial Fears:

SEPARATE FEELINGS, THOUGHTS, FACTS, AND ACTIONS

✓ Use the following worksheet to help sort through the feelings and thoughts surrounding the financial fallout from your crisis, and distinguish them from the facts. Then identify some concrete actions you can take that will help you manage the situation based on these facts. Use the example as guidance. You may find yourself having different negative thoughts based on different emotions, or experiencing multiple feelings within one dominant thought.

FEELINGS	THOUGHTS
For example, fear; anxiety about the future.	I can't afford to get my son the care he needs. We're going to have to sell everything and I'll never be able to retire.

Notes:

FACTS	ACTIONS
My son needs to be in the hospital for three weeks and that will cost between $15,000–$20,000.	I can contact my insurance company to find out my expected share of costs. I can call the hospital to work out a payment plan. I can take money out of savings and retirement savings to pay these bills.

CHAPTER TWO

BEGINNING WITH YOUR STARTING POINT

It may sound obvious, but to repair and restore your financial health, you need to begin with your starting point. That means taking a deep look at your current financial snapshot, from your monthly expenses to the balance in your 401(k) to the $50 your brother owes you. You can't make a workable plan that will allow you to take meaningful money steps if you don't have a clear picture to start from. These first steps can feel impossible, but breaking them down into smaller pieces that you can easily handle will help you get it done.

In this chapter, you'll pull together information about your current financial situation. That will include things like identifying new costs related to the crisis, analyzing your current cash flow, and taking inventory of the resources you already have in place that can help cover those costs. Again, though, you'll want to limit your focus to one thing at a time. The same goes for making decisions, which you'll prioritize so you can make one at a time. As you're able to check things off of your financial recovery to-do list, you'll gain momentum, and your financial picture will come into focus. With the insights you'll get from having all of your information together, it will be much easier to create and follow your recovery plan. It all starts here.

Gather All of Your Financial Facts

When your situation is filled with uncertainty, you need to start with facts. You may be worried that it's too overwhelming to look at your big-picture finances during a crisis, but it will actually give you a sense of comfort and control. When you know where you are, it's easier to map out a route of where you want to go.

This process will take a while, so try to block off some chunks of time when you can really focus on putting all of this information together. The worksheets at the end of this chapter will give you direction and help you get your financial facts organized so you can use them as a springboard for your financial recovery. Fill them out in order, and work on one at a time rather than trying to multitask. You want to make sure nothing gets overlooked here, because these worksheets will provide the support for your entire recovery journey. In the following sections, you'll learn more about the steps to gathering your own financial facts, and which worksheets will help you complete each step.

STEP 1: CRISIS-SPECIFIC COSTS

The first thing you'll need to do is pinpoint the specific expenses tied directly to your crisis situation. These temporary costs don't figure into your normal budget, but they will play a huge part in your crisis budget. For example, during a health emergency, you'll not only need to consider the extra costs of medical care, but also things like transportation and special foods. The Ongoing Crisis Costs worksheet at the end of this chapter will help you think of every cost you could be facing until your situation gets resolved. This worksheet has a different section for each type of emergency. While some expenses may be common to several different situations, each crisis comes with unique costs, some that may not be so obvious.

New emergency costs that many types of financial crises have in common include:

- Increased childcare
- Therapy
- Legal fees
- Taxes
- Health insurance premiums

Most crisis-specific costs will disappear after a while, but some—like therapy or insurance premiums—may need to be folded into your ongoing budget.

STEP 2: CASH FLOW

Next, you'll need to know your current cash flow. That involves a combination of how much money is moving in and out and the timing of those movements. The Current Cash Flow worksheet at the end of this chapter will help you determine these different factors. To get a good sense of timing, you'll list out your income and expenses by week, which will help you match up money in and money out. On the incoming cash portion of this worksheet, you'll include only money that you're *guaranteed* to receive. But on the outgoing cash portion, you'll list every possible expense that you could need to pay, including the ongoing crisis costs you tallied up in the first step.

This worksheet is not the same as a budget, and it might show more money going out than coming in for some weeks. That's to be expected as you start to work on your plan and make adjustments to cover the additional temporary expenses and account for things like lower paychecks if your crisis calls for a lot of missed work time.

Many people stuck in the middle of a financial crisis turn to credit cards to cover household expenses, even if that's not something they'd normally do. It can be a good way to maximize cash flow and meet your essential expenses during the crisis, as long as you make sure to stick to your budget. Using credit cards can make it easier to inadvertently overspend unless you do it mindfully and according to plan. That can help you make sure that you don't end up dealing with expensive credit card debt long after your emergency situation has passed.

STEP 3: NET WORTH

After you've got a good handle on your current cash flow, you'll want to use the Know Your Net Worth worksheet at the end of this chapter to take a look at your net worth—a snapshot of where you stand right now, financially speaking. This will help you clarify your current financial position and identify the resources you have to work with. Basically, calculating your net worth involves adding up everything you own, then subtracting everything you owe— sort of like your financial inventory. Don't worry if your net worth comes up negative. That's very common, especially for people:

- At the beginning of a career
- Paying off student loans
- Going through major life changes, like having a child
- Dealing with a crisis that affects their finances

Net worth gives you a way to measure progress and take stock of your financial situation at any time. And while the current crisis can drive down your net worth, your plan to weather the situation will include steps to increase it over time.

Two major life changes—death and divorce—may directly affect retirement assets. It's crucial to make sure that retirement accounts are handled properly in these situations, because if they're not, you could end up facing some huge tax consequences on top of everything else.

With divorce, both sides of the retirement equation call for careful treatment. If you are the spouse splitting your retirement savings, make sure to get a *properly executed* QDRO (qualified domestic relations order) from the court. This ensures that you will not have to pay state and federal income taxes on the withdrawal, and you won't be hit with a 10 percent early withdrawal penalty. Without a proper QDRO you will have to pay both, and that can add up to a huge amount of money lost to taxes.

If during a divorce you're the spouse receiving retirement funds, you will face tax consequences if you don't put that money into your own retirement savings. If you decide not to directly roll over the distribution into a retirement account, the plan manager will normally withhold 20 percent for federal income taxes. The exception to this is if the money you got came from a Roth IRA. If you need the money now, it's okay to not put it into a retirement account—just be prepared for the tax hit so you can plan accordingly.

If you inherit an IRA from a deceased spouse, you have two choices: You can put the money into your own retirement account, or keep it separate as an inherited IRA. The choice you make here affects whether and when you'll *have to* start taking money out of the account as RMDs (required minimum distributions). If you want to keep the money in a tax-sheltered retirement account for as long as possible, you'll want to roll it over into your own IRA. That will keep the money locked up until you turn at least fifty-nine and a half, and you won't have to take any RMDs until you turn seventy-two. If you want access to the money now, transfer the funds into an inherited IRA account. You'll have to take at least the RMD every year—you can take more if you want to—and you won't have to pay a 10 percent early withdrawal penalty no matter how old you are. You will have to pay regular income taxes on any money, including the RMD, that you withdraw from the inherited IRA.

> ### A 50 Percent Penalty!
> If you skip an RMD or don't take enough money, the IRS will charge you a penalty equal to 50 percent—half!—of the money you didn't withdraw. If you have a "reasonable" reason (such as illness, natural disaster, or death in the family) for not taking the full RMD, you can request a penalty waiver from the IRS *after* you fix the missing RMD.

If you inherit an IRA from someone other than a spouse, your only option is to create an inherited IRA account in your name. You will have to take RMDs every year, and must take all of the money out of the account within ten years. The money you take out won't be subject to early withdrawal penalties no matter how old you are, but you will have to pay regular income taxes on the withdrawals. These rules apply even for Roth IRAs, which normally do not have RMDs.

STEP 4: DEBT TABLE

The final piece of your financial facts puzzle is an in-depth look at your current debt load. This isn't the same as the debt portion of your net worth. It's a closer look at all of the details tied to each individual debt. You can gather this information from your original loan documents and current loan or credit card statements.

In the Debt Table worksheet at the end of this chapter, you'll categorize your debt by type, such as:

- Mortgage or home equity
- Student loans
- Auto loans
- Personal loans
- Money owed to friends or family
- Credit card debt
- Medical debt

You'll also list all the details for each debt, so you have the information all in one place when you need it. Those details include things like the current outstanding balance, the interest rate, and the contact information for the lender.

Make One Decision at a Time

When you're facing dozens of decisions, your ability to make choices can disappear and leave you feeling stranded. Instead of looking at your entire decision to-do list, focus on one item at a time. Yes, many of these decisions will be interconnected, but that doesn't mean you can't tackle one piece before moving on to the next. You don't want to get burned out here, because that can lead to complete avoidance of your financial situation.

You'll find that making one decision will lead you to the next. With each choice you make, you'll gain more confidence and control, and that will make future decisions less stressful. With choices that seem impossible to make, try talking them through with someone else or breaking them down into even smaller pieces.

You've already made at least one positive choice: You got this book, and you're using it as a framework to develop your financial recovery plan. Filling out the worksheets will provide clarity and direction that can help you make the decisions you're facing. And it is important to make decisions—sooner rather than later. A slightly wrong move is better for your finances than making no moves at all, so don't strive for perfect; aim for "this could work."

The key here is to not freeze up and shut down (I know that's harder than it sounds). Fear of making wrong decisions, especially when they might affect your family's financial security, can be paralyzing. That's why you'll stick with one decision at a time, so you can pivot if things don't turn out the way you expect. Plus, you'll have a wealth of information from the worksheets in this book to help you make these choices. That makes you more likely to come up with the best possible solutions for your financial health.

PRIORITIZE YOUR DECISIONS

Before you start making financial decisions, create a list of the things you need to decide—even things that aren't necessarily financial decisions. As you start jotting them down, you'll see how one choice may lead to or depend on others. Making a sort of "decision tree" will help you see how all the decisions are interconnected and also give you a sense of the best places to start. This method can also help you spot potential trade-offs, conflicts, and deadlines well in advance.

As you work through this book, you'll uncover information that will help you make the best decisions, ones that take your current situation and your future security into account. Prioritizing your decisions will also help clarify your options and solidify your choices, so you'll know you're making the right ones.

TAKE A HOLISTIC APPROACH

A lot of people struggling through financial setbacks get stuck in tunnel vision. They focus only on cutting costs or minimizing debt rather than looking at their whole situation. That narrow focus can be disheartening, especially during a crisis situation where you have less control over your finances than you normally would. Balancing offensive moves (such as bringing in more money) and defensive moves (like slashing expenses) can get you through more quickly—and feel more rewarding—than taking a one-sided approach. The best way to achieve a complete financial recovery here involves taking a holistic look at your full financial picture and taking steps that serve your overall finances rather than one piece at a time.

Consider Professional Help If Things Feel Overwhelming

When you're going through a crisis and are trying to deal with the financial fallout at the same time, it's easy to get overwhelmed. That feeling can lead you to shove the money problems to the bottom of your to-do list or even ignore them altogether. But skipping over these issues can make them worse. So if you just can't manage this part of your situation on your own, get help.

Spending even one hour with a financial professional can be well worth your time. Some of the ways they can help include:

- Reducing the stress surrounding the financial picture
- Figuring out ways to improve cash flow
- Sorting through bills and obligations with you so you don't have to face them alone
- Taking an objective look at your net worth and debt
- Suggesting strategies to simplify your financial task list
- Make sure your tax returns get filed on time to avoid penalties and speed your refund

And if you really just can't manage this part of your situation, an experienced and sympathetic financial professional can take at least part of the burden off of your to-do list. You may feel like you need to do this all on your own—like you can't justify spending money on something you think you could do yourself. But consider this: Taking care of yourself and your family is priority one, and nothing at all will get done if you are burned out.

Take It from a CPA

During my financial crisis, I hired someone to do my taxes and also sat down with a financial planner. Even though both of those things are normally part of my job, I needed someone outside of my situation to help me handle them. Yes, it added expenses when money was already tight. But handing off those tasks also reduced my stress level a lot, which allowed me to keep moving forward and get my finances back under control.

Farm out what you can—even if you have to pay for it—to help you through to the other side of this situation.

WHICH PROFESSIONALS CAN HELP YOU?

Different pieces of your situation call for different types of professionals, so consider building yourself a financial recovery team. The professionals you'll enlist depend somewhat on the kind of crisis that set off your financial setback. For example, if you're dealing with health-related issues, you might want to include someone who can help you navigate and negotiate with insurance companies and care providers.

Core members of your financial recovery team could include:

- **Financial coach:** to help you gather your financial facts and come up with a workable plan
- **Financial planner:** to help you define and meet big-picture financial goals
- **Certified public accountant (CPA) or tax preparer:** to help you minimize the tax impact of your emergency financial choices
- **Investment advisor:** to help you figure out which retirement and non-retirement investments to sell—and when—to minimize damage to your long-term finances

- **Financial therapist:** to help you come to terms with the strong emotions tied to this situation
- **Medical billing advocate:** to uncover billing mistakes and incorrect insurance company denials and negotiate with providers on your behalf
- **Insurance agent:** to help you file claims and deal with your insurance providers

Some professionals may straddle categories, like a CPA who also offers financial coaching services. Others, like medical billing advocates, are highly specialized and focused. No matter who you add to your crisis team, keep the communication flowing and coordinated. You want everyone moving in the same direction.

HOW DO YOU FIND LEGITIMATE AND RELIABLE PROFESSIONALS TO WORK WITH?

It can be hard to find the right financial professionals when you're in the middle of a crisis. You don't have the time or energy to sort through dozens of possibilities, but you absolutely don't want to choose someone randomly. These relationships can make your journey easier to bear...or complicate things even more.

If you already work with any financial professionals, fill them in on your situation. Someone who's familiar with at least a piece of your financial picture can offer immediate guidance and may be able to refer you to other types of advisors. If you've always been a do-it-yourself person and don't currently work with anyone like this, pick the type of professional you think you need most (most people start with some kind of financial coach) and start your search there.

Your team selection to-do list should include:

- ☐ Checking credentials and licenses
- ☐ Verifying experience in helping people through financial recovery
- ☐ Meeting with every candidate at least once before hiring anyone
- ☐ Asking for and checking references (if not through a direct referral)

Make sure you choose people you feel completely comfortable with. You'll be working closely with every member of this team and dealing with tough issues. You need to feel safe, heard, and in control. If you have any doubts or something feels off, choose someone else. The state of your current and future finances is too important to be working with someone you can't be open with or don't fully trust.

HOW MUCH SHOULD YOU HAND OFF TO SOMEONE ELSE?

When you're overwhelmed, one of the best things you can do is delegate as much as possible. That's true here too, but with a caution: You need to understand and participate in every financial decision. For example, you can enlist a financial coach to help you complete all of the worksheets in this book, but don't have them do it all for you. These worksheets will give you a firm grasp on your financial picture, immediate and long term, and you need that knowledge in order to create and stick to your recovery plan.

Basically, you want to hand off tasks but not control. Keeping control over all decisions and financial moves will keep you involved without bogging you down. You are the key to your financial recovery, especially when it comes to sustaining long-term financial health.

ACCEPT HELP WHEN IT'S OFFERED

Even if it might feel a little weird or uncomfortable to accept financial help, you need to do everything you can to help yourself and your family weather this financial setback. If it will help you accept money from someone, create a simple loan document and call the assistance a bridge loan that you'll pay back when your finances are in better shape.

Let yourself welcome help in any form, whether it's free childcare, extra work, a few meals, or actual cash. Accepting help means you recognize that you're struggling, and you're savvy enough to use every possible resource that comes your way.

Chapter Worksheets

The following worksheets will help you gather the information needed to begin making decisions and plans to weather your crisis. Visit https://michelecagancpa.com/FinRec101 for downloadable versions (password: F1n@nc!@LRec0very!).

ONGOING CRISIS COSTS

✅ Think about the new ongoing costs you may face due to your current situation. List them here, then add them to your crisis budget.

EMERGENCY	EXPENSE	BUDGET
Health Crisis		
	Medicine	
	Medical supplies	
	Recurring outpatient visits	
	Transportation and travel for care	
	In-home care	
	Childcare	
	Hospital stay(s)	
	Therapy	
	Other	
Divorce		
	Legal fees	
	New housing costs/replacing basic home necessities	
	Utility bills	
	Refinancing mortgage or car loan (account for higher monthly payments)	
	Health insurance premiums	
	Child visitation travel	
	Childcare	
	Therapy	
	Other	

Death

Legal fees

Outstanding debt payments

Medical bills

Health insurance premiums

Tax payments

Childcare

Therapy

Other

Job Loss

Job search costs

Career counseling

Employment agency

Health insurance premiums

Estimated tax payments:

Income tax on unemployment

Income and self-employment tax

On gig work or freelancing

Life insurance

Therapy

Other

Natural Disaster

Emergency travel

Temporary housing costs

Rebuilding and repairs

Medical expenses

Replacing basic necessities

Childcare

Therapy

Other

CURRENT CASH FLOW

✅ Use this worksheet to track when and how much money flows into and out of your household. For cash coming in, include only money that you can count on 100 percent. For cash going out, include every expense you may need to pay. Timing matters here, so do your best to list each item by week. Don't worry if your cash out is greater than cash in right now. This worksheet lets you know how much cash you have to come up with or borrow and can help you see if some expenses will need to be delayed.

As this worksheet is specific to one month, you will need to make at least six copies and fill out at the start of a new month in your crisis. You can also find a downloadable version at MicheleCaganCPA.com.

MONTH:

CASH COMING IN	WEEK 1	WEEK 2	WEEK 3	WEEK 4
Net Paycheck				
Insurance Money				
Side Gig Income				
Investment Income				
Social Security				
Alimony/Child Support				
Business or Rental Income				
Other				
Total Cash Coming In	$	$	$	$

CASH GOING OUT	WEEK 1	WEEK 2	WEEK 3	WEEK 4
Rent/Mortgage				
Utilities				
Food and Household Supplies				
Medical:				
Health Insurance Premiums				
Medicine				
Doctor Visits				
Auto Expenses:				
Gas				
Maintenance				
Insurance				
Car Payment				
Professional Fees				
Taxes				
Alimony/Child Support				
Ongoing Crisis Costs				
Other				
Other				
Other				
Total Cash Going Out	$	$	$	$

DEBT TABLE

✓ Use this worksheet to list the details of your debts.

TYPE OF DEBT	NAME OF LENDER OR CREDITOR	CONTACT PHONE NUMBER	CONTACT EMAIL ADDRESS

REMAINING BALANCE	MINIMUM MONTHLY PAYMENT	PAYMENT DUE DATE	INTEREST RATE

Total: $

KNOW YOUR NET WORTH

✅ This worksheet will help you calculate your net worth to provide clarity to your current financial situation. First, you'll list all of your assets, which are the resources you have to draw from. Next, you'll list all of your debts. Your net worth equals your assets minus your debts, and that result tells you where you stand financially right now.

ASSET: WHAT YOU HAVE	$ AMOUNT
Cash (include savings and checking)	
Investments	
Retirement Accounts	
House (current market value)	
Car (current trade-in or resale value)	
Other	
Total Assets	$

DEBT: WHAT YOU OWE	$ AMOUNT
Mortgage	
Home Equity Loan or Line of Credit (HELOC)	
Car Loan	
Student Loan	
Credit Card Debt	
Personal Loan	
Medical Debt	
Other	
Total Debts	$

ASSETS	– DEBTS =		NET WORTH
$	– $	=	$

Notes:

CHAPTER THREE

CREATING A PLAN TO MOVE THROUGH THE CRISIS

When you're smack in the middle of a crisis, creating a financial escape plan may not land on your to-do list. But working out a plan now will actually free up both money and mental space to help you cope more easily during this difficult time. Follow the guidelines in this chapter to fill in the provided worksheets and create your plan. We'll start with what you need to do for immediate survival and lay out the steps necessary to help you cope financially with the current crisis while doing the least possible damage to your long-term finances.

Carve out some space, even if it's just ten or twenty minutes per day, to work on your plan. Tackle as much as you can handle each day until you have a manageable plan in place. As you begin to take control of the financial piece of your circumstances, you'll start racking up accomplishments that can boost your confidence and reduce your stress levels. Every time you complete a worksheet or check off a financial task, you'll get a little dopamine rush (it's science) that acts like a mental reward. You can also build rewards into your plan to help you acknowledge your triumphs and encourage you to keep going. Because that's the way out of this financial quicksand: filling out the worksheets, making a plan, mapping out your steps, and following them until you're back on solid ground.

Rethink the Rules

General personal finance rules typically include pretty standard advice:

- Build up emergency savings
- Max out retirement account contributions
- Aggressively pay down debt
- Spend less than you earn

That's good advice, typically, but not when you're in the middle of a financial crisis. In your current circumstances, the rules get flipped upside down. Now, cash and access to financial resources (like credit cards) are the priorities. You're in survival mode here, and anything that doesn't contribute to that can wait.

During a financial crisis, your true needs come into sharp focus: home, food, medicine, transportation. Expenses necessary for survival take priority. Long-term goals, like paying down debt or saving for a house, take a back seat to immediate needs. That can be frustrating, but it's only temporary. Your crisis plan will still address debt and savings goals—they'll just be lower priority than your survival needs.

As you move through the crisis, your overall finances may take a hit. That's to be expected, and it's okay. You may run through your savings. You may have to sell off investments (even if that means selling at a loss). Your debt load may increase. Remember, all of these are temporary and necessary. Your longer-term financial goals will be put on pause, but they won't disappear if you go into this with a solid plan.

Follow Your New Financial Rules

Now that you've set aside general financial advice, the new rules you'll follow as you move through this crisis are:

- Preserve cash at all costs
- Stop saving for retirement or long-term goals
- Stop paying down debt above minimum payments
- Negotiate to lower or pause debt payments wherever possible
- Keep your credit cards active (even if you don't *need* them yet) to avoid cancellation or limit reduction
- Apply for increased credit limits or additional credit cards (especially 0 percent interest cards)

These are the kind of steps you need to take to maximize your access to resources. Until the crisis is resolved, you don't know how long it will take or how much you'll need to weather it. So you need to create enough financial space to carry you through for as long as possible.

> ### Take It from a CPA
>
> When I lost my job, I immediately applied for a new credit card with a 0 percent introductory rate and got my credit limits increased on the cards I already had. I didn't know whether I'd need to use that credit or not, but I wanted to make sure I had it just in case. It turned out to be a very smart move. I used the new card to pay for my health insurance premiums, a huge new expense related to the job loss.

This mental shift may feel uncomfortable—it did for me and most of the people I've worked with during financial crises. That discomfort is not a bad thing. It's more like a reminder that you want to return to more positive financial habits. And don't let it—or anyone—stop you from doing whatever you need to do to get through this difficult time.

DEALING WITH SUDDEN LOSSES

Crisis losses can happen in two ways: physical losses and/or paper losses, and both can be devastating. With physical losses, tangible property that you own—real estate, a car, your belongings—gets destroyed or disappears. With paper losses, the *market* value of assets you own—like your house, a rental property, or a stock portfolio—drops dramatically, but you still have those assets. The best way to handle sudden losses depends on which type of loss you've endured.

Physical Losses

Fires, floods, and natural disasters can damage or completely wipe out your property. These situations are extra difficult if you're forced to evacuate your home at a moment's notice, without time to grab even your most basic necessities—let alone important papers.

While you're figuring out where to go, what to do, which things you'll replace, and how to cope, there are some steps you can take to protect yourself and your remaining property:

1. Do what you can to secure your property, especially a home, against further damage.
2. File an insurance claim as soon as you possibly can in any way that you can: Call your insurance agent, send an email, or start the process online.
3. Talk with your insurance agent about your coverage and what you need to do for your claim.
4. Ask your insurance company for an advance, have the insurance company deliver it to you wherever you're staying right now, and keep all the receipts for replacing your essentials.
5. Keep copies of everything you submit to insurance, take detailed notes of conversations, save original copies of

invoices and estimates, and gather all of this information in a single place (like a binder).

6. Don't stop paying your insurance premiums, especially homeowners insurance, which still covers you and your belongings while you're forced to stay elsewhere.

7. Consider hiring a public insurance adjustor to negotiate with your insurance company for you, potentially increasing your settlement for a fee. You can find a public adjustor on the National Association of Public Insurance Adjusters website at www.napia.com.

Don't Close Your Claim Too Soon

Do *not* accept a check from your insurance company that says "in full release of" until you're 100 percent sure you're ready for the claim to be closed out. It may take months before you discover all of the damages and losses you've sustained. If you need the money now, cross out those words and initial the change *before* you deposit the check. Send the insurance company a polite letter stating that you don't believe the claim is closed and are happy to continue working with them.

I know this can feel like a lot. But it's important to take these steps before it's too late to get the full payout you and your family deserve. Take it one thing at a time, and you will have a solid list of steps completed in no time.

Paper losses offer you at least some control. These losses don't lock in until you actually sell the assets that have lost value, though they can cause severe financial distress. For example, if your home value drops below your outstanding mortgage balance, you'll be "underwater" on your mortgage—meaning you couldn't pay off your loan by selling your house. And if you rely on your investments for income, whether or not you're fully retired, seeing a dramatic drop in market value can have a chilling effect on both your immediate income and your future prosperity. The best thing to do if you've sustained paper losses is to wait them out, if that's possible. Market values almost always rebound over time—so if you can stick this out, you can come out ahead.

If your current situation doesn't allow you to sit tight and you have to sell sooner than you'd like, there are things you can do to minimize your losses. With an underwater home, you could:

- Move somewhere cheaper and rent out your house
- Rent out a room, garage, shed, or other space
- Increase your home value with do-it-yourself or low-cost upgrades

In addition, if your mortgage is through Freddie Mac or Fannie Mae, you may be able to refinance through their assistance programs. Find information about the Freddie Mac Relief Refinance Mortgage—Open Access at sf.freddiemac.com, and about the Fannie Mae High Loan-to-Value Refinance Program at www.fanniemae.com.

When your investment portfolio has suffered substantial market losses, take a look at your individual holdings. If you have investments that were performing poorly before the market decline, consider selling them and at least benefiting from the related losses for tax purposes (a strategy called "tax loss harvesting"). Hold on to investments that fit in your portfolio plan before the market declines, as they will almost certainly rebound in value given enough time. Work with an investment advisor to come up with the best possible plan to preserve as much of your portfolio as possible.

Special Steps with Identity Theft

If your finances have been hurt by identity theft, you're not alone. The FTC (Federal Trade Commission) received 3.2 million reports of identity theft and fraud in 2019 alone, and those numbers have been climbing steadily for years. If you've been a victim, you need to take specific steps to limit your losses and begin your financial recovery:

1. Call all of the companies where fraud took place. Explain that your identity was stolen, ask them to close or freeze your accounts, and change all of your passwords and PINs.
2. Put a free fraud alert in place by contacting any one of the three main credit bureaus (the one you contact has to inform the other two): Experian, TransUnion, and Equifax.
3. Get free copies of your credit reports from all three bureaus.
4. Report the identity theft or fraud to the FTC by completing the online form at www.ftc.gov/contact or calling them at 1-877-438-4338.
5. Report the crime to your local police department and file a police report.

You can find more information about dealing with identity theft at www.identitytheft.gov.

Refocus Your Goals

If you've been making progress toward financial goals, it can feel frustrating and discouraging to stop—and even worse to back-track. So although your long-term goals are on hold, they haven't disappeared entirely. You just have to shift your focus toward the immediate problems right now. Right now you want to regain financial security and stability; that's it.

Your new goals are straightforward:

1. Cover essential expenses
2. Cover noncritical needs
3. Avoid tapping in to retirement funds
4. Avoid taking on debt

It may be impossible to meet all of these goals, especially at first, but covering essential expenses gives you at least a little space to figure out your next moves. Use the Crisis Financial Goals worksheet at the end of this chapter to help you clarify and track your new goals.

Plan for a Short-Term, Bare-Bones Financial Crisis Budget

During this crisis, your income and expenses may be unpredictable, and that can make it harder to plan. That's why you'll need to take some extra steps to prepare your budget, so you can make sure that at least your most essential expenses get covered every month.

Creating a crisis budget involves some sacrifice, but it's important to remember that this is a short-term plan. You just need to make some big temporary changes that will help you get through until your financial situation stabilizes. Once that happens, you'll be in a prime position to rebuild your finances and increase your long-term financial security and wealth.

STEP 1: PRIORITIZE YOUR EXPENSES

The first step toward creating your crisis plan involves prioritizing your expenses. Use the Expense Priority worksheet at the end of this chapter to list all of your regular monthly expenses. Make sure to add in any new expenses you're dealing with because of the emergency. Remember to include space for expenses you pay only occasionally, using the Periodic Expenses Calendar worksheet at the end of this chapter.

As you're completing the expense worksheets, you'll rank each expense based on how much you honestly need it to survive. There's no judgment involved in the rankings: Look at your expenses with an objective eye to see which ones you really need now and branch out from there.

Here's what my expense priority rankings look like (your priorities may look different than these examples, but you get the idea):

Rank 1: Essential expenses necessary for your family's life and health, including things like:

- Mortgage or rent
- Food
- Utilities (electricity, water, phone, Internet access)
- Medicine and immediate-need medical care
- Transportation (essential travel only: work, medical, school)

Rank 2: Necessary but noncritical expenses involving security, stability, and loss prevention, including things like:

- Insurance (health, life, auto, homeowners/renters)
- Minimum debt payments
- Clothing (mainly for growing children)
- Routine medical and dental care
- Car repair and maintenance
- Childcare

Rank 3: Unnecessary for right now (things you'll want to add back when you can), including things like:

- Emergency savings
- Retirement savings
- Aggressive debt payment
- Previous savings goals that still apply
- Memberships and activities that you regularly participate in
- Paid apps and streaming services (if you have kids, these may fall under Rank 2)

Rank 4: Unnecessary things you could do without in the long term, including things like:

- Memberships you don't use
- Multiple streaming services
- Household help (cleaners, landscapers, dog walkers, etc.)
- Dining out and entertainment

Your Rank 1 expense total will show you how much money you absolutely must come up with to survive each month. If you can cover only Rank 1 expenses right now, that's okay. That will get your family through the next month or two, giving you a little room to figure out your next steps. Depending on your resources, you may be able to add in some or all of the Rank 2 expenses, which will help preserve your financial security as much as possible.

STEP 2: IDENTIFY YOUR CASH RESOURCES

Once you've completed the expense worksheets, you'll work on figuring out how much money you have to use with the Cash Resources worksheet. You'll list everything that you could use to pay for your expenses here, but it has to be *guaranteed access*. Do not include money you expect to get at some point or loans and benefits you need to apply for. This worksheet is for money you could turn to right now to buy groceries or pay rent.

Make sure to include every possible resource that you could access. Examples of cash resources include things like:

Cash Coming In:

- Regular salary income (from all the jobs you have)
- Unemployment
- Social Security benefits
- Existing side gig (that's already bringing in more money than it costs)

Assets You Can Use:

- Savings
- Investment accounts
- FSAs and HSAs
- Roth IRA
- Traditional retirement accounts (IRA, 401(k), 403(b), etc.)

How to Use Your FSA and HSA Funds

If you have any money in an FSA (Flexible Spending Account) or HSA (Health Savings Account), use it to pay for qualifying expenses. Just keep in mind there are strict limits on what you can use it for: only IRS-approved medical expenses or eligible childcare costs (with child-care FSA accounts). *Use your FSA funds first*, because if you don't use all of that money, you lose it at the end of the year. If you've already paid for some medical expenses out of pocket, request reimbursement from your FSA or HSA from the administrator.

Money You Could Borrow with Minimal Hassle:

- Home equity line of credit
- Credit cards (available balance, not credit limit)

Hopefully, you won't have to go too far down the list to cover your essential expenses. But if you do, don't worry: You'll have time to recover, replenish, and repay once your financial life gets back to normal.

STEP 3: KNOW YOUR COVERAGE

Once you have your expenses and resources sorted out, you'll put them together to create your crisis budget. Unlike a standard budget, this crisis budget is for the short term—just the next thirty days. After that, your financial picture could look very different, so you may need to reevaluate it. Financial crises are unpredictable and often include factors beyond your control. So keep an immediate focus—just for now—until your situation stabilizes.

Hopefully, you have some dependable cash coming in that can cover at least a portion of your critical expenses. If not, make your way down the list (in order of priority) until you have the essentials handled for the upcoming month. Either way, you'll assign every dollar coming in to a specific expense to make sure your critical needs are paid for.

If You Have Enough Current Income for All Rank 1 Essentials

If your current income is greater than your Rank 1 expenses, move on to Rank 2 expenses. If you can cover all of those as well, that's great. If not, prioritize your Rank 2 expenses in order of their importance to your family's stability and security. For example, health insurance premiums top a no-issues six-month dental cleaning (if you have to pay out of pocket for it).

If all of your Rank 1 and 2 expenses can be covered with income, and you still have some income left over, put *all of it* into emergency savings. During this first crisis month, I do not recommend putting cash toward any Rank 3 priorities except for emergency savings. The others can come back into play once your situation has stabilized. For now, accessible cash is king.

If you're in a situation where you no longer have enough money coming in to cover your essential expenses, you have five options:

1. **Reduce essential expenses.** During this first month, you may not be able to reduce essential expenses, but you might be able to delay some. While I wouldn't normally recommend using credit cards for household expenses you couldn't cover with cash, doing that can help stretch out available cash during a crisis. Stick to the bare minimum you need, but consider paying for food, gas, and medicine with your lowest-interest-rate credit card. If you can pay any of your utility bills with credit, do that too. Again, this might feel super-uncomfortable, but it's only for this month to give you some cash breathing room. See Chapter 5 for more details.

2. **Increase current income.** Increasing income may call for some mental and emotional reshuffling, especially if you've lost your job and can't find comparable work. It can feel weird to take a gig delivering pizzas or walking dogs, especially if you're coming from a managerial or high-level position. But you need to bring in money any way you can right now—whatever it takes to cover your essential bills. See Chapter 4 for more details.

3. **Use emergency savings.** If you have emergency savings, this is exactly what they're for. This is the time to dip into this money. It can feel very unsafe to pull money out of an emergency fund, and using this money can bring on anxiety. After all, if you use it all up, you won't have a safety net anymore. But right now, the situation you're in calls for a safety net. And pulling from emergency

savings beats not paying the rent, going into debt, or taking money out of investment or retirement accounts.

4. **Raid investment and retirement accounts.** Once emergency savings have been depleted, you can turn to your non-retirement investment accounts. Yes, you may end up owing taxes if you sell investments, but it's also possible that doing this will lower your tax bill. Plan carefully before taking money out of retirement accounts. If you do this the wrong way, you'll lose 10 percent of your cash off the top (in IRS penalties) *and* owe income taxes on the withdrawal. You'll find safe withdrawal strategies for this in Chapter 4. This step can feel especially uncomfortable if your crisis involves a sudden loss in asset value and you've already retired. If you have a drawdown plan in place for your retirement accounts, try to follow it as closely as possible.

Your Best Move Here

Talk with a trusted financial advisor who can help you figure out the best strategy to maximize the amount of cash you'll get while minimizing the long-term impact on your finances. Even if you normally manage your own investments—retirement or otherwise—this is a different situation. It will help to have an objective professional look at what you have, what's going on in the markets, and what the tax fallout might be.

---

5. **Take on new debt.** We've already talked about putting essential expenses on credit cards to preserve cash, and that's a reasonable strategy when you're in the middle of a financial crisis—but it may not be enough. Before you're too far in, before your credit score starts to take a hit, you may want to borrow some money if you can. That could include getting additional credit cards, requesting more available credit on existing cards, borrowing against your

house with a home equity loan or home equity line of credit (HELOC), or getting a personal loan. Like some of the other recommendations here, this is not standard financial advice—in fact, it's the exact opposite. But right now you need to increase your resources as much as possible, and that can include taking on debt. If you do this before you start missing bill payments, you'll be able to get better terms than you would if you waited until your credit score dropped. By waiting until you really need to borrow money, you may not be able to get reasonable interest rates from reputable lenders. So if you think you're going to need to borrow money, *do it now*. It will only be harder later.

The sooner you take the steps necessary to cover your essential expenses, the easier it will be. You'll end up using a combination of these strategies, so don't worry about doing them "out of order." The most important takeaway here is to find a way to pay your essential expenses right away, and everything else can wait.

Stay Flexible and Adjust Your Crisis Budget As Needed

When you're in the middle of a crisis, you'll start expecting the unexpected, especially when it comes to your finances. Things can change rapidly during an emergency situation, and every change adds a new dimension to the financial picture. That's why your plan has to be flexible and allow for frequent shifts in income and expenses.

If a monthly budget becomes hard to maintain, switch to a weekly or even daily budget until your situation settles down enough to stretch back out. If your income varies—like it does for freelancers, small business owners, and people who work on commissions—you may not know how much money you'll have available ahead of time. It's okay to update your budget as money comes in or a new expense crops up.

Your plan won't be perfect. It may not even be complete at first. That's okay. It's more important to start taking action immediately than it is for your plan to be "right." You'll be able to make corrections as you go, so don't get bogged down in creating the *best* plan. All you need right now is a workable plan, and one that lets you start taking steps ASAP.

How to Handle Unpredictable Income

When your paycheck fluctuates week to week or your income comes from self-employment sources, use the least amount you honestly expect to receive for your guaranteed income. Treat any amount more than that as probable income, but don't count on it to meet your essential expenses.

Remember: Your crisis budget is a tool for you to use, not a reminder that you're in financial trouble. Its job is to let you know how much money you need each period to cover your most essential expenses. You need to know if you can't cover your rent or your usual grocery bill this month, because knowing that information is the only way to figure out how much more money you need and come up with a plan to get it.

Celebrate Every Victory

It can be hard to find the motivation to keep going during a crisis situation that puts a huge drain on your finances. That's why it's so important to celebrate your wins, no matter how small they seem, and give yourself credit for every goal you meet.

Honestly, acknowledging even the smallest victories can help keep you going. That's because your brain releases a feel-good chemical called dopamine when you perceive success, and it gives you a little dopamine rush (I'm not making this up—it's real science). Dopamine works like a reward for your brain, and it propels you forward in search of the next win. That energizing effect can go a long way toward helping you stay focused and motivated during this journey to financial recovery.

Not sure what counts as a win? Here are some examples:

- Reading a chapter in this book
- Completing a worksheet
- Finding one resource
- Getting professional help
- Making one decision
- Breaking even on your monthly budget
- Negotiating a lower amount for a bill
- Getting a good deal on something you need
- Spending less than you expected to
- Setting a goal
- Meeting a goal
- A month you don't add new debt
- A month you don't take money out of retirement savings
- Adding anything to savings

Anything that feels like a victory to you is one. So however you decide to celebrate your wins—I go with chocolate—do it every time.

All of these smaller victories will add up, and soon you'll start to see big, positive changes in your financial situation. And when you're back in a strong, healthy financial position, treat yourself to something wonderful. You deserve it.

Chapter Worksheets

The following worksheets are designed to help you map out and follow your crisis financial plan. They provide the details you need to move through each step and determine which choices make the most sense for your situation. Tackle one piece of information at a time, and soon you'll have the full picture laid out in front of you. Downloadable Excel spreadsheets for each worksheet can be found at https://michelecagancpa.com/FinRec101 (with the password F1n@nc!@LRec0very!).

EXPENSE PRIORITY

✔ Enter one month's expenses on each line.

RANK 1 EXPENSES	$ AMOUNT
Rent or mortgage payment	
Food	
Medicine	
Essential/urgent medical care	
Utilities:	
Gas and electric	
Phone	
Water	
Internet	
Transportation:	
License and registration	
Gas	
Essential repairs and maintenance	
Total Rank 1 Expenses	$

RANK 2 EXPENSES	$ AMOUNT
Childcare	
Minimum debt payments	
Clothing	
Insurance:	
Health	
Auto	
Homeowners/renters	
Life	
Routine medical and dental	
Routine car repair and maintenance	
Total Rank 2 Expenses	$

RANK 3 EXPENSES	$ AMOUNT
Emergency savings	
Aggressive debt repayment	
Retirement savings	
Savings goals	
Memberships	
Paid apps	
Streaming services	
Activities fees	
Total Rank 3 Expenses	$

RANK 4 EXPENSES	$ AMOUNT
Dining out and entertainment	
Multiple streaming services	
Household help:	
Cleaners	
Landscapers	
Dog walkers/pet sitters	
Other	
Memberships you don't use anymore	
Total Rank 4 Expenses	$

Notes:

CASH RESOURCES

✅ Enter total available cash on each line.

RELIABLE CASH COMING IN THIS MONTH	$ AMOUNT
Net Paycheck(s)	
Social Security/Social Security Disability Insurance (SSDI)	
Pension	
Unemployment	
Investment Income (interest and dividends)	
Side Gig/Freelancing/Consulting*	
Rental Income	
Royalties	
Total Cash Coming In	$
ASSETS YOU COULD PULL CASH FROM	**$ AMOUNT**
Savings	
CDs (certificates of deposit)	
Money Market Accounts	
Flexible Spending Accounts (FSAs)	
Health Savings Accounts (HSAs)	
Non-Retirement Investment Accounts**	
Savings Bonds	
Roth IRA**	
Traditional Retirement Accounts:	
*IRA***	
*401(k)***	
*403(b)***	
Whole (Permanent) Life Insurance Policy	
Total Quick-Cash Assets	$

MONEY YOU COULD BORROW WITH MINIMAL EFFORT	$ AMOUNT
Advance on Paycheck	
Credit Card Available Balance:	
Credit Card 1	
Credit Card 2	
Credit Card 3	
Credit Card 4	
Home Equity Line of Credit (HELOC)	
Home Equity Loan	
Friends and Family	
401(k) or 403(b) Retirement Account	
Total Borrowing Potential	$

*Include only side gig income you reasonably expect to collect this month.
**Use the account value on the day you complete this sheet, knowing those values may change.

Notes:

PERIODIC EXPENSES CALENDAR

✅ Use this to capture expenses you pay only occasionally. Enter the amount due in the applicable month(s).

PERIODIC EXPENSE: AUTO INSURANCE

JAN:	FEB:	MAR:	APR:
MAY:	JUN:	JUL:	AUG:
SEP:	OCT:	NOV:	DEC:

Total Periodic Expense $

PERIODIC EXPENSE: CAR REGISTRATION

JAN:	FEB:	MAR:	APR:
MAY:	JUN:	JUL:	AUG:
SEP:	OCT:	NOV:	DEC:

Total Periodic Expense $

PERIODIC EXPENSE: DRIVER'S LICENSE RENEWAL

JAN:	FEB:	MAR:	APR:
MAY:	JUN:	JUL:	AUG:
SEP:	OCT:	NOV:	DEC:

Total Periodic Expense $

PERIODIC EXPENSE: ROUTINE CAR MAINTENANCE

JAN:	FEB:	MAR:	APR:
MAY:	JUN:	JUL:	AUG:
SEP:	OCT:	NOV:	DEC:

Total Periodic Expense $

PERIODIC EXPENSE: DENTAL CHECKUP/CLEANING

JAN:	FEB:	MAR:	APR:
MAY:	JUN:	JUL:	AUG:
SEP:	OCT:	NOV:	DEC:

Total Periodic Expense $

PERIODIC EXPENSE: ROUTINE VETERINARIAN CARE

JAN:	FEB:	MAR:	APR:
MAY:	JUN:	JUL:	AUG:
SEP:	OCT:	NOV:	DEC:

Total Periodic Expense $

PERIODIC EXPENSE: PROPERTY TAXES

JAN:	FEB:	MAR:	APR:
MAY:	JUN:	JUL:	AUG:
SEP:	OCT:	NOV:	DEC:

Total Periodic Expense $

PERIODIC EXPENSE: SCHOOL SUPPLIES/CLOTHES

JAN:	FEB:	MAR:	APR:
MAY:	JUN:	JUL:	AUG:
SEP:	OCT:	NOV:	DEC:

Total Periodic Expense $

PERIODIC EXPENSE: TUITION

JAN:	FEB:	MAR:	APR:
MAY:	JUN:	JUL:	AUG:
SEP:	OCT:	NOV:	DEC:

Total Periodic Expense $

PERIODIC EXPENSE: BIRTHDAY AND HOLIDAY EXPENSES

JAN:	FEB:	MAR:	APR:
MAY:	JUN:	JUL:	AUG:
SEP:	OCT:	NOV:	DEC:

Total Periodic Expense $

PERIODIC EXPENSE: ESTIMATED TAX PAYMENTS

JAN:	FEB:	MAR:	APR:
MAY:	JUN:	JUL:	AUG:
SEP:	OCT:	NOV:	DEC:

Total Periodic Expense $

PERIODIC EXPENSE: OTHER

JAN:	FEB:	MAR:	APR:
MAY:	JUN:	JUL:	AUG:
SEP:	OCT:	NOV:	DEC:

Total Periodic Expense $

CRISIS FINANCIAL GOALS

✓ Use this template and the provided examples to create your own crisis-related financial goals. Make your goals as specific as possible so it will be easier to reach them. Wherever it makes sense, include dollar amounts and time frames or deadlines. Right now, you may not know how you'll meet these goals, so you can add goals that include figuring things out.

EXAMPLES OF CRISIS-RELATED GOALS		
FINANCIAL GOAL	**$ AMOUNT**	**DEADLINE**
Increase my monthly income by $500 within six weeks.	$500	Within six weeks
Find three ways to either reduce essential expenses or bring in extra money so I can cover $3,150 in essential expenses every month during this crisis.	$3,150	Within sixty days
Complete the worksheets in this workbook so I can make a plan to manage my crisis finances.	N/A	Within three months
Negotiate with my creditors to reduce my total debt payments to under $1,500 per month.	under $1,500	Within three months
Find a trusted financial advisor by March 1 to help me clarify and manage my financial situation.	N/A	By March 1

MY GOALS		
FINANCIAL GOAL	**$ AMOUNT**	**DEADLINE**

LONG-TERM DEBT MANAGEMENT

✅ Complete this worksheet to determine the best ways to minimize the current cash burden of your debt. Use the following list of possible debt strategy options as you fill in the worksheet.

- Forbearance (F)
- Deferment (D)
- Interest-only payments (IO)
- Minimum payments (M)
- Reduced payments (R)
- Loan modification (LM)

Notes:

TYPE OF DEBT	CURRENT MONTHLY PAYMENT	STRATEGY (F, D, ETC.)	NEW MONTHLY PAYMENT	STRATEGY END DATE
Mortgage				
Mortgage				
Home Equity Loan				
Student Loan				
Student Loan				
Student Loan				
Auto Loan				
Auto Loan				
Personal Loan				
Home Equity Line of Credit (HELOC)				
Credit Card				
Credit Card				
Credit Card				
Credit Card				
Credit Card				
Payday Loan				
Short-Term Loan				
Total Monthly Cash Out for Debt	$			

SHORT-TERM CRISIS BUDGET

☑ This "upside-down" budget is designed to help you make sure you have your essential expenses covered. Pull information from your previous Expense Priority and Cash Resources worksheets. Include only the expenses for this month.

MONTH:	
ESSENTIAL (RANK 1) EXPENSES	**$ AMOUNT**
Rent or mortgage payment	
Food	
Medicine	
Essential/urgent medical care	
Utilities:	
Gas and electric	
Phone	
Water	
Internet	
Transportation:	
License and registration	
Gas	
Essential repairs and maintenance	
Total Essential Expenses	$
FIRST CASH RESOURCES	**$ AMOUNT**
Total Reliable Income Sources	
HSA and FSA	
Total First Cash Resources	$
DIFFERENCE*	$

*If difference is positive, move to Additional Expenses. If difference is negative, move to Additional Resources.

Notes:

ADDITIONAL EXPENSES	$ AMOUNT
Childcare	
Insurance:	
Health	
Auto	
Homeowners/renters	
Life	
Minimum debt payments	
Clothing	
Routine medical and dental	
Routine car repair and maintenance	
Total Additional Expenses	$
DIFFERENCE✱✱	$

✱✱If difference is positive, put that money in emergency savings for next month. If difference is negative, remove any expenses that can be put off until next month until the difference is zero.

ADDITIONAL RESOURCES✱✱✱	$ AMOUNT
Savings	
Money market accounts	
CDs (certificates of deposit)	
Investments (non-retirement)	
DIFFERENCE	$

✱✱✱List savings based on your Savings Management worksheet (see next section) until the difference hits zero. If difference is still greater than zero, decide whether to borrow money or use retirement savings this month.

SAVINGS MANAGEMENT

✓ Use this worksheet to map out the most efficient use of your savings. (Refer to the Types of Savings and Possible Withdrawn restrictions keys to help you fill it out.) Create your drawdown plan to minimize the drain on your savings and maximize earnings. Pull from the lowest earnings rate sources first. Consider withdrawal fees as part of this factor. Remember to consider any tax consequences.

NAME OF SAVINGS ACCOUNT	SAVINGS TYPE (R, CD, ETC.)	EARNINGS RATE

Types of Savings:
- Regular Savings Account (R)
- Certificates of Deposit (CD)
- Money Market Accounts (MM)
- Investment Accounts/ Non-Retirement (I)

Possible Withdrawal Restrictions:
- Interest Penalty
- Number of Withdrawals
- Amount of Withdrawals

CURRENT BALANCE	WITHDRAWAL RESTRICTIONS	WITHDRAWAL FEES	TAX ON WITH-DRAWALS? Y/N

CHAPTER FOUR

FINDING WAYS TO BRING IN OR FREE UP MORE MONEY

You can only reduce your expenses so much, and many of them you won't be able to reduce at all. That leaves increasing cash inflows as your main option for adding space to your crisis budget. When you're in the middle of a crisis, the thought of pounding the pavement to bring in more money may seem like a nonstarter. But you may have more available resources and options than you realize.

In the following chapter, you'll learn more about each of these resources and options, and determine which ones are the best fit for your situation. Now is the time to get creative, and finding cash sources includes much more than trying to work longer and harder with limited time and energy. Some options may make you feel uncomfortable, but don't immediately dismiss those ideas. Right now, the main objective is taking care of yourself and your family financially without sacrificing your entire financial future. That might include doing things that you wouldn't normally do, like applying for Supplemental Nutrition Assistance Program (SNAP) benefits or selling off your possessions. And as unappealing as that can seem (I know—I've done both), it will make things easier right now and help you recover faster financially.

Cover Crisis Costs and Dig Out of the Financial Hole

It can seem so difficult to avoid getting stuck in a deep financial hole during a crisis situation, but you can do it if you create and stick with a plan. Your first move here will be figuring out ways to cover your new monthly expenses using as little debt as possible—especially high-interest-rate debt. You have two main ways to come at this: Reduce outgoing cash and expenses (which may not be possible), or increase incoming cash (which can be tough when you have limited time and energy).

You'll want to get the biggest benefits for your efforts here. For example, reducing one large expense (like a car payment) takes less energy than trying to trim a dozen small expenses. On the flip side, taking a minimum-wage part-time job will suck up much more of your time and energy than figuring out a way to earn more money in less time. That may sound impossible, but it's not, especially if you take the time to figure out your best moves rather than taking the first available option out of fear. Fill out the Skills Inventory and Networking Contacts Inventory worksheets at the end of this chapter. You may find that you have more marketable skills than you realize, and that you know a lot of people who could connect you with better-paying jobs.

What you need here is breathing room—enough extra coverage from your incoming cash that you aren't forced to borrow more money than you'll be reasonably able to pay back. If working more and reducing expenses can't get you there, tap in to other resources so you can make ends meet without burning yourself out.

MINE YOUR FORGOTTEN OR HIDDEN RESOURCES

Most people have resources that they overlook when it comes to finances. That could be anything from $20 in your winter coat pocket to credit card points to an old gift card that you've never used.

Happy Birthday!

I had one client who found a stack of old birthday cards from their grandparents, all containing varying amounts of money. They ended up finding more than $200. While that didn't cover their entire budget gap, it made a big dent, and that was $200 less they charged on a credit card.

So where should you start looking for resources you don't even remember you have? Everywhere. Start with physical places you may have absentmindedly stashed some money: old wallets, pocketbooks, pants and coat pockets, change jars. Look through your closets for clothes (or other items) you forgot to return—even if you can't find the receipt, many places will let you at least exchange sealed items and clothing with tags or get store credit. Another potential jackpot: savings bonds. According to Executive Order 13968 "Promoting Redemption of Savings Bonds," the US government estimates that there are more than seventy-five million unredeemed savings bonds floating around for an estimated total of $27 billion.

The next step: Look at your credit card statements to see if you've built up rewards points. You may be able to use those points to pay down the related credit card bill, but you'll often get a better deal by spending them. That doesn't mean random spending on things you don't need. But many points programs will let you buy gas, groceries, and gift cards for stores like Target, where you can buy household essentials.

Follow that up with an "unclaimed money" search—just in case. When businesses, government agencies, banks, and other entities owe you cash that you don't collect, that money is considered unclaimed. That includes state and federal income tax refund checks that were never cashed or deposited, credit balances on accounts with companies (like if you returned something for a store credit), and old bank accounts that you forgot about. Start your search online at www.usa.gov/unclaimed-money or www.missingmoney.com. You never know what you might find!

Other sources for increasing your cash resources may include:

- Selling household items that you don't use
- Selling ad space on your car through apps like Carvertise, Wrapify, or StickerRide
- Using, trading, or selling old gift cards
- Selling old clothes—including clothes your kids outgrew— online through *ThredUp* or *Poshmark*

Use the Hidden Cash Resources worksheet at the end of this chapter to tally up both instant cash and quick cash potential (from selling things). Don't dismiss things that add only a few dollars to your cash flow. This all adds up, and finding even a few extra dollars means less struggling right now.

THIS IS WHY YOU HAVE EMERGENCY SAVINGS

If you have emergency savings—or any other non-retirement savings, for that matter—this is the time to use them. It can feel very uncomfortable to burn through your safety net. But even if you do use up all of your savings here, you will be able to restore and increase them once the crisis situation has passed, as long as you do all of this with a clear plan.

A lot of people I've worked with feel like it's safer to use credit cards than to raid their savings. I can understand that feeling, but the financial facts don't support it. Building up credit card debt will cost more in the long run and make it harder to recover financially. Using savings first works better for your total financial picture. Once your savings gets depleted, then you'll consider borrowing to cover your essential expenses until the immediate crisis has been handled.

Take It from a CPA

At first, it made me feel sick to my stomach to pull money out of my emergency savings to cover my regular household expenses. The specific expenses didn't feel like emergencies, and I felt like that money was for blown tires or sick pets. But my whole situation was a financial emergency—I just had to force my brain to see it that way. It didn't make draining my savings feel completely comfortable, but it did stop making me feel sick.

Look back at your Savings Management worksheet in Chapter 3. That will give you the bones of your savings drawdown plan and outline the best order and timing for withdrawing that money.

SELL NON-RETIREMENT INVESTMENTS FOR QUICK CASH

If you have non-retirement investments, such as stocks or mutual funds, you can cash in your holdings at any time. It might take a few days before the transactions clear and money lands in your account, so plan the timing of any security sales to mesh with your outgoing payment due dates. In most cases, you will have to pay fees, such as transaction or brokerage fees, to sell securities, so make sure you factor those into your budget.

It's a good idea to talk to an investment advisor before you decide which investments to sell. If you decide to do it yourself, it generally makes sense to sell off securities or funds that are performing poorly and that you don't expect to rebound. That gives you the triple benefit of stopping losses, getting cash you need to cover the essentials, and either reducing the amount of taxable gains or delivering tax-saving losses.

If you do make money selling your investments, you will have to pay capital gains taxes, but not at the time of the sale. On the plus side, these gains are typically taxed at much lower rates than the income that you work for. In some cases, that tax rate may even be zero.

You can also withdraw dividends and interest from investment accounts rather than reinvesting them. Since you pay taxes on these earnings every year whether or not you take the cash, it won't add to your tax bill to cash out current earnings.

THE BEST WAY TO TAP IN TO RETIREMENT FUNDS

Normally, I tell people flat out to leave their retirement accounts alone. After all, imagine going through what you're dealing with now when you're eighty-five. That said, if pulling from your retirement savings is the only way you can stay afloat without taking on crippling high-interest debt, use this money. But make sure to do it in the smartest way possible.

If you're younger than fifty-nine and a half, you'll have to pay a 10 percent penalty if you withdraw money from your retirement accounts. That's 10 percent on top of the regular income tax hit you'll face for taking money out of a traditional retirement account like an IRA, 401(k), or 403(b) plan. Here's what that looks like:

Suppose you withdraw $10,000 from your IRA. You'll immediately be hit with a 10 percent penalty, which drags your cash down by $1,000. On top of that, the custodian (the company that holds your IRA) will probably automatically withhold 10 percent of federal income tax, pulling another $1,000 out of your cash.

So, you're already down to $8,000, plus you'll owe state income taxes and possibly additional federal income taxes (depending on your tax bracket). Out of that $10,000 withdrawal, you may only end up keeping around $6,000—much less than the amount you need.

By withdrawing that money in a specific way, you'll be able to minimize the tax hit and possibly avoid the early withdrawal penalties. That's why it's a good idea to work with a financial advisor or a tax professional to help you figure this out. Generally speaking, though, there is a cash-preserving order and key methods for using retirement funds.

Potential Source 1: Roth IRA

With Roth IRAs, you've already paid taxes on the money you put in. That means you can take it out at any time without paying any penalties or additional taxes, making it the best first choice if you're planning to tap in to retirement money. But if you withdraw any *earnings*—meaning anything more than the money you contributed—both taxes and penalties will come into play. So be very careful when you take money out of your Roth IRA. That means you should know exactly how much money you've contributed before you take money out, so you can avoid owing anything to the IRS.

Potential Source 2: Borrowing from an Employer-Based Plan

If you are *currently working* and have money in your employer-based retirement plan, usually a 401(k) or 403(b) plan, contact your plan administrator to find out if you can borrow money from your account. Borrowing offers some clear advantages over straight withdrawal but also comes with some big potential drawbacks. When you borrow money, there's no tax impact and you get to pay the money back with interest, which can help reduce the drain on your retirement savings. On the downside:

- Payments will be taken directly from your paycheck, usually starting with the paycheck immediately following the loan
- Most plans don't allow you to make contributions while a loan is outstanding, which can affect your savings plans once the crisis has passed
- If you leave your job for *any reason* (including being fired), you'll have to pay the loan back in a lump sum, or it will be converted to taxable early withdrawal

You'll want to think carefully before going with this option. Even though borrowing from your 401(k) sounds like a great idea, it can have unintended consequences that will impact your future finances.

Potential Source 3: Withdrawing from Traditional Retirement Accounts

If you need to withdraw money from traditional retirement accounts, remember to take out more money than you need. You'll lose a *minimum* of 20 percent of your withdrawal to federal income taxes and IRS penalties, often right off the top. So, for example, if you *need* $10,000, you'll have to withdraw $12,500.

Be aware that not all employers allow early withdrawals from 401(k) plans, and that may include hardship withdrawals. Check with your employer to find out whether you can take money out of your account this way before you include it in your plans. If they don't, consider rolling over a portion of your 401(k) into a traditional IRA where you'll have more control over the money.

It's also important to note that Roth 401(k) plans work differently than traditional 401(k) plans, and there are different rules for withdrawing from a 401(k) plan if you are seventy-two or older.

When it comes to Roth 401(k) plans, you can withdraw money that you put in (if your employer allows) without taking a tax hit. But to make a tax-free *qualified* withdrawal that exceeds your contributions, you have to be at least fifty-nine and a half and have started contributing to the account at least five years before. Anything else counts as an unqualified withdrawal, which will be subject to income taxes and possibly a 10 percent early withdrawal penalty.

Once you reach the age of seventy-two, the IRS required minimum distribution (RMD) rules force you to start withdrawing from your traditional (meaning not Roth) retirement accounts every year. The RMD calculation is based on the value of your retirement account and your life expectancy according to the IRS. If you have multiple retirement accounts, you have to figure out the RMD for each one separately every year. *But* you don't have to take money out of every account. You can add up all of your RMDs for the year and take them out of whichever account (or accounts) that you want. And while you can't withdraw *less* than your total annual RMD from your retirement accounts, you can take out more money.

So, here's the retirement account withdrawal strategy to use if you're seventy-two or older:

1. Take your RMDs
2. Take distributions from Roth IRAs
3. Go back to your traditional retirement accounts for a double dip if you need additional funds

You can find out more about RMDs, including how to calculate them, on the IRS website at www.irs.gov/retirement-plans.

Consider Extra Work Options

When you're trying to bring in more money as quickly as you can, earning through work tends to be the first go-to. And while it can bring in fast cash, you'll need to pay attention to the drain on your energy and the potential increase in your stress levels as well. Under this umbrella, you have three options:

1. **Overtime:** working more hours for pay at your current job (if you can).
2. **Multiple jobs:** either full-time or part-time.
3. **Side gigs:** self-employed options that offer more flexibility than traditional jobs.

All of these choices call for a time commitment and could possibly add to your expenses as well. For example, you may need to pay for additional childcare, transportation costs, or takeout meals. Since your available time and money will be more limited during a crisis situation, make sure that this extra work doesn't end up costing you too much of either to be worthwhile. The point here is to add financial space and reduce financial stress, so make sure to consider the whole picture when looking at these options.

HIGH-PAYING PART-TIME JOBS

If you're going to add a part-time job, it's worthwhile to go for one that pays more than minimum wage—and hopefully a lot more. At the same time, you want this side job to offer at least some flexibility, especially if your particular crisis demands a lot of your time. To make this worth your while, you'll want this extra work to add enough to your monthly cash flow that you won't need to find a third or fourth way to bring in cash. Ideally, it will cover your entire shortfall.

It may sound like a fantasy, but there are part-time jobs like this out there. You just have to know which types of jobs to look for. Higher-paying, flexible part-time positions include:

- **Social media marketer:** create and schedule social media posts for small business owners. These gigs typically take up to five to seven hours per week, and as of 2021 average a salary of $1,000–$1,500 per month.
- **Customer service representative:** respond to customer calls and direct them to solutions for their problems. As of 2021, CSRs can earn $15–$20 per hour working flexible hours from home.
- **Bookkeeper:** manage a company's everyday accounting tasks such as recording transactions and paying bills. Part-time bookkeepers can earn $18–$40 per hour (as of 2021) depending on where the company is located.

You can find opportunities like these and more by searching online at websites like *FlexJobs* (www.flexjobs.com) and *Indeed* (www.indeed.com). You can also sign up with a temp agency, either online or in person near you, to find temporary jobs that will help fill in your budget gaps.

SIDE GIGS YOU COULD START TODAY

The gig economy has exploded in recent years, and apps make it quick and easy to get started. With so many options available in this realm, you should take the time to figure out what would be simple for you to do—something that won't require a lot of training or too much effort on your part. Use the Skills Inventory worksheet at the end of this chapter to list your existing skills, which probably include more than you realize.

Many side gigs require a time (and sometimes money) investment to get started. The ones listed here don't; you can start them right away by just signing up on an app. Instant side gigs include:

- Delivering groceries through apps like Instacart, DoorDash, and Postmates
- Driving for a rideshare service with Lyft or Uber
- Helping people move with Dolly
- Doing chores and handyman stuff with TaskRabbit, Thumbtack, or Handy
- Dog walking and/or pet sitting with Rover, Wag!, or Fetch!
- Babysitting with apps like Care.com, UrbanSitter, or Bambino

With any of these, you can pick and choose which gigs you want to take, working around your schedule and responsibilities. You'll work when you want and get paid quickly. Although you won't be guaranteed gigs (or pay), this kind of work can be better for your situation because you won't be tied to a specific schedule that you may not be able to meet (depending on your specific crisis).

Understand That More Income Means More Taxes

Whether you sell investments, pull money from retirement accounts, or work more hours to bring in money, you will have to deal with taxes. And the more money you bring in, the more you'll owe. That can be especially tricky when no tax gets taken out of the money you get, and you're expected to make quarterly lump-sum payments to the IRS. While taxes may not be an immediate concern, they are part of the picture, so you don't want to ignore them completely. The following sections explore the different kinds of taxes you'll face and how you can pay them.

If you work with a CPA or other tax professional, talk with them about the best ways to manage potential tax issues before you take action. They may be able to offer invaluable advice that can help you avoid taxes and tax penalties simply by following specific IRS guidelines, especially when it comes to taking money out of retirement accounts.

IF YOU SELL NON-RETIREMENT INVESTMENTS

Any time you sell investments, you'll see a tax effect. When you sell them for a gain—meaning you sell them for more than you originally paid for them—you'll owe capital gains taxes on the difference. If you sell for a loss, that will first be used to offset any capital gains you have, and then up to $3,000 in losses can go toward reducing your total taxable income. Any leftover losses (greater than $3,000) can be carried over to the next year's tax return.

The tax rate depends on how long you've had the investment. For tax purposes, any investment that you've had for more than one year counts as long term. Long-term capital gains get taxed at lower rates than short-term gains. So if you're coming up on that one-year mark, *wait* before you sell, if that's at all possible. The tax difference will be worth it.

IF YOU TAKE MONEY OUT OF RETIREMENT ACCOUNTS

The taxes on retirement account withdrawals depend on three things:

1. Your age
2. The type of retirement account
3. The type of withdrawal

There are also three main types of *nontaxable, penalty-free* withdrawals:

1. Taking a loan from your 401(k), as long as you pay it back as directed
2. Taking your own contributions out of a Roth IRA at any age
3. Taking earnings (any amount more than your own contributions) out of a Roth IRA when you're at least age fifty-nine and a half *and* have had the account for at least five years

Most other withdrawals will trigger income taxes, tax penalties, or both. However, you may be able to get penalties waived due to financial hardship or IRS exceptions. Different exceptions apply to different types of retirement accounts but generally include:

- Permanent disability
- Qualified higher education expenses
- Qualified first-time home buyers (up to $10,000)
- Some unreimbursed medical expenses
- Health insurance premiums paid while you're unemployed

Visit the IRS website at www.irs.gov for a more complete discussion on how retirement account withdrawals will affect your income taxes.

FOR 1099 CONTRACTORS AND GIG WORKERS

When you earn money by working, you pay both income taxes and self-employment (or payroll) taxes: Social Security and Medicare. Normally, payroll taxes are split 50/50 between an employee and their employer. But when you work as a contractor, freelancer, consultant, side-gigger, or as any type of 1099 worker, you count as both the employee *and* the employer because you are technically self-employed. That means you have to pay both parts of payroll taxes, a total of 15.3 percent of your income, and that's on top of regular federal and state income taxes.

In order to reduce all of those taxes, make sure to deduct every single work-related expense from your self-employed income. You couldn't do that as an employee, but as an employer (of your-self), you totally can—you are a business, after all, at least for tax purposes. You can deduct everything from work-related mileage to Internet access to office supplies (basically anything you spend to produce that income). The IRS has a complete list of deduct-ible business expenses for self-employed people on their website at www.irs.gov.

FOR EXTRA JOBS WHERE YOU GET A PAYCHECK WITH TAXES TAKEN OUT

When you're working for a regular paycheck, you can maximize your take-home pay by minimizing the amount of withholding taxes taken out. To do that, you'll fill out a new Form W-4, which you can get from the HR or accounting department at work, or on the IRS website at www.irs.gov. You may want to play around with a withholding tax calculator to help you figure out which fields to fill in and how, in order to reduce your taxes and increase your net pay. The IRS has a free app on their website that walks you through all of the factors that affect your take-home pay.

IF YOU GET UNEMPLOYMENT

The federal government and most states tax unemployment benefits just like any other income. If you don't get taxes withheld, you will owe more at tax time. You can request federal income tax withholding by filling out and submitting IRS Form W-4V (Voluntary Withholding Request) to the agency in charge of your state's unemployment system. Some state agencies have their own version of the form, so check their website before you submit.

WHEN AND HOW TO MAKE ESTIMATED TAX PAYMENTS

Almost every time you bring more money into your household, you'll have to pay federal and state income taxes on it. When those taxes don't get taken out of your income—like you see on regular paychecks with withholding taxes—you have to proactively make quarterly payment to the IRS and your home state instead. But since you're doing this to increase your cash on hand, you'll want to keep the most cash possible right now. That might mean skipping or delaying *making* estimated tax payments for as long as possible, even it that ends up triggering tax penalties and a bigger lump-sum tax payment down the road.

Still, whether or not you decide to make estimated tax payments, it's important to get a sense of how much you'll owe so you can start making plans to deal with it. Your total amount due for estimated tax payments may include three different types of taxes: income tax, capital gains tax, and self-employment tax. Self-employment tax will only come into play with 1099 income or if you have your own business that's not a corporation. Capital gains tax will come into play when you sell investments for more money than you paid for them. Regular income taxes may apply to:

- Retirement account distributions
- Non-retirement investment earnings, such as interest and dividends
- Self-employment income (in addition to the payroll taxes)
- Unemployment

Remember that you may also have deductions and credits that will lower your taxable income, so take those into account before you come up with your estimation.

Use the Estimated Taxes worksheet at the end of this chapter to come up with your expected tax burden. Alternatively, if you used tax software (such as TurboTax or TaxAct) to do your taxes last year, it probably came with a worksheet for estimated taxes that you can use this year. You can also use the worksheet included as part of IRS Form 1040-ES (available at www.irs.gov), the form you'll use if you file and pay estimated taxes by mail. Visit your state's website to find out their process for calculating and making estimated tax payments.

Once you have your estimated taxes figured out, you can decide whether you want to pay them and when. The more you owe and the longer you wait, the more likely you are to face tax penalties, which you can probably get waived due to your financial situation. And when money is tight, it makes sense to put at least the bulk of these payments off until you file your annual tax return and deal with any penalties then. If you do decide to make an estimated payment, the easiest way to do that is online at www.irs.gov for federal income taxes, and on your state website for state taxes.

Use Caution When Borrowing

When cash is tight and bills are piling up, borrowing money—and that includes credit card spending—may be your only option. But for the protection of your current and future financial situation, you want to be very careful when you do this for three important reasons:

1. Everything you buy with that borrowed money will cost more because of interest.
2. The more credit you use, the lower your credit score will sink, making future borrowing more expensive.
3. You'll build up debt, which will eat away at your net worth and financial resources.

This isn't to say that you shouldn't borrow money when you need to. But when you *do* borrow, do so armed with complete information and a plan. Do some research and find your best options for borrowing, which will be unique to your situation. While doing your research, you'll have to take some key factors into account, such as:

- **Timing:** how fast do you need the money.
- **Amount:** how much money you reasonably expect to need (see more on this later in this chapter).
- **Existing available credit:** room left on credit cards and HELOCs.
- **Interest rates:** on both your existing options (like credit cards) and potential borrowing options (like personal loans or home equity loans).
- **Credit score:** your credit score may affect your access to new funds and will certainly impact how much you'll pay (in interest) to borrow more.
- **Payments:** when the payments will start and how much space they'll claim in your already tight budget.

If borrowing money offers more help than harm to your situation, it makes good financial sense. But if the opposite is true, and it will make your current situation even harder to manage, look for another option. For example, if repayments start immediately and will make your budget tighter, borrowing that money would not be a good choice.

TAKE CAREFUL ADVANTAGE OF NO- OR LOW-INTEREST PROMOTIONS

If you can get a no-interest or extremely low-interest credit card promotion, get it. These options can help you manage your emergency finances without a huge interest buildup as long as you handle them the right way. If you don't, there's a terrible downside that erases all the benefits of having the card at all.

If you're going to use this card for spending, make sure to only use it to cover essential expenses. Even if monthly payments are not required, make them on the card to keep the balance from becoming unmanageable. Look for the lowest-rate card with the longest possible promotion period. You'll need to pay the balance in full before the promotion ends in order to avoid getting charged a lot of interest. In most cases, any unpaid portion will get tagged with interest retroactively, meaning as if it were a regular high-interest card the whole time.

You can also use these for balance transfers to get rid of at least some high-interest-rate debt. This can free up a lot of space in your budget, because high-rate debt takes up a lot of cash and gives you nothing back. If you do balance transfers, *do not use the same card for spending.* If you do, every payment you make will go toward your purchases and not toward the balance you transferred. That means your balance will not be paid down as quickly as you planned. And, again, you'll be charged interest on the remaining balance from the day you did the original transfer.

Bottom line: If you get a promotional rate for a credit card, make a concrete plan to pay your balance in full before the promotional period ends. If you don't, it could end up costing you more than you can handle.

HOW MUCH SHOULD YOU BORROW?

The answer to this question during a crisis is different than it would be in a noncrisis situation. Right now, you need to maximize your borrowing, because your future ability to borrow may be limited even more by the situation. Over time, your credit utilization (the percentage of your available credit that's used up) will almost certainly increase, and your ability to cover payments may decrease, both of which will drag your credit score down.

As I mentioned previously, my grandmother often said that "everything takes longer and costs more than you expect." And she was right, especially when it comes to crisis situations where you may have limited—or no—control over things that affect your finances. However much money you think you'll need to borrow, add at least 10 to 20 percent more. If you don't need to use that money, you can pay it back early. But it's better to have access to cash you don't need than need cash you can't access.

When you're figuring out how much money you'll need, remember to include your regular monthly expenses, costs that crop up periodically (like car insurance that you pay twice a year), and the extra expenses brought on by your particular crisis. Consider how long you may be facing extra expenses and reduced income opportunities, as this also plays a part in figuring out how much money you'll realistically need to borrow. For example, if you know you won't be able to work full-time for at least six weeks, make sure you borrow enough to last you at least that long. Use the How Much Should I Borrow? worksheet at the end of this chapter to help clarify both the amount of money you think you'll need and the extra 10 to 20 percent, and create a realistic outline of how you'll begin to pay that money back.

WHAT ABOUT PAYDAY LOANS?

While I would normally strongly advise against high-interest short-term loans like payday loans, if that is your best or only option, you may need to borrow that way. The important part here is to borrow with a payback plan already in place, or you could get sucked into revolving debt quicksand that's extremely difficult to escape. That's because when you finally get your paycheck, you have to hand it over to the lender, leaving you with no money and the need to roll over your payday loan. This rollover process happens repeatedly, and it's nearly impossible to break out of the borrowing cycle.

While not all payday loans involve predatory lenders, many do. The difference here is disclosure. Predatory lenders actively hide facts about their loans from the borrower. If the lender you're considering tries to gloss over loan terms, leaves anything blank in the contract, or pressures you into signing, leave. There are dozens of alternatives out there, and you can find a lender that's up front about the loan costs.

No matter which payday lender you use, the interest rate on this loan will be extremely high, often 300 to 400 percent annually and charged up front. For example, a $30 loan charge for a $100 loan works out to 30 percent interest just for that month, or 360 percent annualized.

If a payday-type loan is your best or only option, get one. Use it as a bridge to cover a temporary gap in your cash flow. Know exactly how much the loan will cost you, and exactly how you will pay it back *without needing a rollover loan*.

If you have the time, financial space, and energy to look at other options, you can find alternatives to ultra-high-interest payday loans. These will still cost you more than regular loans but won't come with the crippling interest rates common to predatory payday loans. When you have a cash gap and need money immediately, consider these other options:

- Get an advance on your paycheck from your employer
- Look at paycheck advance apps like Chime (www.chime .com), PayActiv (www.payactiv.com/employees), or Branch (www.branchapp.com)
- Borrow money from friends or family using a signed note and a detailed payback schedule that you will be able to stick to in your current circumstances
- If you belong to a credit union, ask about payday alternative loans (PALs), which are specifically designed to help you pay them off

If you can tap in to any of these alternatives, do it. They will do far less damage than a regular payday loan. And if that does turn out to be your only option, go into it with a plan so you don't fall into a hard-to-break loan rollover cycle.

Know Where to Look for the Help You Need

There's a lot of assistance available for people facing financial struggles—you just have to know where to look. Unfortunately, navigating aid resources can feel like a walking through a maze trapped inside a puzzle. That's especially true when it's your first time trying to find your way through. In addition to getting help from friends, family, and community, you can find assistance through federal, state, and local government programs and private aid organizations. Your search will start in different places depending on your unique situation and the type (or types) of aid that would be most helpful for you.

Don't avoid searching for aid because you think you might make (or have made) too much money to qualify. Many programs don't have income qualifications, and others will only take into account your current situation.

Check into government assistance programs using Benefit Finder (www.benefits.gov) to find agencies that will help you make ends meet during this crisis period. This online questionnaire gathers some information, supplies you with a list of benefits that you qualify for, and directs or connects you straight to the agency that will provide the aid. Those benefits may include:

- Unemployment
- Disaster relief loans
- Education loans
- Job training
- Childcare resources
- Crime victim compensation
- Temporary assistance with living expenses

- Health and life insurance
- Food and grocery assistance
- School breakfast and lunch programs
- Home energy assistance

Your home state and county also offer a wide variety of assistance programs, some that you'll be connected with through the federal Benefit Finder and others that you'll find on your state's website.

You can also look into nongovernment assistance, which is widely available across the United States. There are hundreds of nonprofit grants and programs that can help with things like housing, out-of-pocket medical expenses, legal assistance, and childcare. One of the best places to start is with Community Action Agencies (CAAs), which often offer several different types of assistance and can help you coordinate resources. You can find your local CAA on the Community Action Partnership website at www.communityactionpartnership.com.

As you begin to seek assistance, use the Resources for Aid Checklist at the end of this chapter to keep a log of what you qualify for and your application status. You may need to follow up, and you'll want a complete record when you do.

Chapter Worksheets

The following worksheets will help you increase the money you have coming in from every possible source. Downloadable Excel spreadsheets for each worksheet can be found at https://michelecagancpa .com/FinRec101 (with the password F1n@nc!@LRec0very!).

SKILLS INVENTORY

✅ When you're looking for a new job or considering a side gig, think about the skills you already have. You have a lot of skills beyond what you did for your last job. Go through the skills and talents listed here and check off everything you can do—whether or not it's associated with a job. You may be surprised by all the skills you have.

Communications Skills

- ☐ Writing reports, letters, and memos
- ☐ Writing stories or poems
- ☐ Reporting news and events
- ☐ Editing
- ☐ Translating
- ☐ Interpreting
- ☐ Public speaking
- ☐ Performing or entertaining
- ☐ Handling complaints
- ☐ Selling products or services
- ☐ Delivering presentations
- ☐ Running a meeting
- ☐ Explaining how to do things
- ☐ Completing forms
- ☐ Taking notes
- ☐ Advising or counseling

Financial and Number-Based Skills

- ☐ Calculations
- ☐ Comparing number data
- ☐ Estimating costs
- ☐ Estimating time to complete tasks
- ☐ Creating spreadsheets
- ☐ Using spreadsheets
- ☐ Creating a budget
- ☐ Managing money
- ☐ Bookkeeping
- ☐ Preparing tax returns
- ☐ Compiling data
- ☐ Analyzing statistics
- ☐ Keeping complete, accurate records
- ☐ Creating charts and graphs
- ☐ Forecasting income and expenses

Management and Leadership Skills

- ☐ Establishing rules and policies
- ☐ Training and teaching others
- ☐ Setting and prioritizing goals
- ☐ Planning
- ☐ Tracking progress
- ☐ Decision-making
- ☐ Delegating tasks
- ☐ Managing and supervising others
- ☐ Motivating others
- ☐ Negotiating
- ☐ Problem-solving
- ☐ Developing and implementing schedules
- ☐ Mentoring
- ☐ Reviewing performances
- ☐ Adjusting and adapting plans
- ☐ Resolving conflicts
- ☐ Organizing events

Technical and Hands-On Skills

- ☐ Construction and building
- ☐ Using tools
- ☐ Electrical work
- ☐ Plumbing
- ☐ Operating machinery
- ☐ Repairing machinery and equipment
- ☐ Installing machinery and equipment
- ☐ Landscaping and farming
- ☐ Skilled crafts
- ☐ Artistic skills
- ☐ Cooking
- ☐ Designing

Notes:

NETWORKING CONTACTS INVENTORY

✅ Whether you're looking for a new or additional job, starting a side gig or small business, or looking for financial advisors, the best place to start is by communicating with people you already know. List all the contacts you have that could increase your networking reach. Add new contacts immediately as they develop. You never know where your next success will come from!

NAME	HOW YOU KNOW THEM	CONNECTED ON LINKEDIN? Y/N	LAST TIME YOU SAW/SPOKE TO THEM
e.g., Nathan	Went to college together	Yes	4th of July at other friend's party

Notes:

WHERE THEY WORK AND THEIR JOB TITLE	PERSONAL INFO THAT CAN HELP YOU CONNECT	NOTES ABOUT CURRENT CONTACT AND FOLLOW-UP
Marketing Manager at XYZ Corp.	Has two dogs, loves pizza; likes sci-fi movies.	Emailed 3/26. Had a Zoom call on 4/2 and will introduce me to the head of accounting. Introduced me to New Connection through email 4/3 and I followed up that day. Waiting to hear back.

HIDDEN CASH RESOURCES

✓ Use this worksheet to help you keep track of resources you forgot or didn't realize were available. With some of these found resources—like money in jacket pockets—you'll have instant access to cash. Others may require you to fill out forms, do online searches, or sign up as an *eBay* seller (for example). Include both instant cash sources and money that will take some effort to recover here.

FOUND RESOURCE	$ AMOUNT
e.g., $2,200 in savings bonds (face value)	$1,750 redemption value
e.g., 34,000 rewards points	$170 statement credit

Notes:

ITEMS TO SELL

✅ Use this worksheet to list of all the household items you're willing and able to sell. Include the amount of money you expect to receive for each item or group of items and how you expect to be paid (for example, in cash or by PayPal). Make a note of the best two places you could sell your items, such as yard sales, pawn shops, *Craigslist*, *eBay*, or the Decluttr app.

ITEM OR GROUP OF ITEMS	EXPECTED SELLING PRICE	PAYMENT METHOD
e.g., ten used video games	$25	cash

Notes:

BEST PLACE TO SELL ITEM	BACKUP SALES VENUE	LISTING DATE	EXPECTED MONEY RECEIPT DATE
yard sale	GameStop	yard sale June 6	June 6

RETIREMENT WITHDRAWAL PLANS

✅ Copy the retirement accounts from your Cash Resources worksheet (Chapter 3) here to get started. Use the first plan if you are under the age of seventy-two. Use the second plan if you are seventy-two or older. List each of your retirement accounts by type.

ACCOUNT NAME	TOTAL CONTRIBUTIONS	ACCOUNT BALANCE
ROTH IRAS		
EMPLOYER-BASED ACCOUNTS, SUCH AS 401(K)S, IF LOANS OR WITHDRAWALS ARE ALLOWED		
TRADITIONAL IRAS		

Notes:

PLANNED WITHDRAWAL	TAXABLE? Y/N	PENALTY? Y/N

Notes:

ACCOUNT NAME	TOTAL CONTRIBUTIONS	ACCOUNT BALANCE
TRADITIONAL IRAS AND EMPLOYER-BASED PLANS		
ROTH IRAS		
DOUBLE DIP: TRADITIONAL IRAS AND EMPLOYER-BASED PLANS ROUND 2		

Notes:

PLANNED WITHDRAWAL	TAXABLE? Y/N	PENALTY? Y/N

ESTIMATED TAXES

✅ Use this worksheet to figure out how much you expect to owe in taxes. These are *estimated* taxes, so it's okay to use *estimated* numbers here. Don't drive yourself nuts trying to be exact!

Step 1: Figure out your total expected self-employment net income	
INCOME/EXPENSES	**$ AMOUNT**
Total income from freelancing, side gigs, and any other 1099 work	
Related expenses like office supplies, parking, and mileage	
NET SELF-EMPLOYMENT INCOME (TOTAL INCOME) – RELATED EXPENSES) =	$
NET SELF-EMPLOYMENT INCOME × 15.3% (SELF-EMPLOYMENT TAX) =	$
Step 2: Add up all of your other expected taxable income from all sources except investment sales	
EXPECTED INCOME SOURCE	**$ AMOUNT**
Paycheck	
Investment income	
Taxable retirement distributions	
Unemployment	
Other	
TOTAL TAXABLE INCOME	$

Step 3: Enter your net total capital gains and losses from non-retirement investment sales	
GAINS/LOSSES	**$ AMOUNT**
If you expect net capital gains, enter your capital gains tax rate from www.irs.gov as a decimal	
Capital gains × capital gains tax rate =	
If you expect a net capital loss, enter the lesser of it or $3,000 as a negative	

Step 4: Add up all of the things that reduce your taxable income (see www.irs.gov for details)	
DEDUCTION	**$ AMOUNT**
50% of the self-employment tax calculated earlier	
Contributions to traditional IRAs	
Educator expenses	
Student loan interest deduction	
Tuition and fees deduction	
Other applicable deductions	
Standard deduction or itemized deductions (see www.irs.gov)	
TOTAL DEDUCTIONS (ADD THESE UP AND ENTER AS A NEGATIVE)	$
Step 5: Determine your expected taxable income	$
Step 6: Calculate your expected total income tax bill using the tax table on www.irs.gov	$

Step 7: Add up all the expected taxes: self-employment, capital gains, and income	$

Step 8: Add up your expected tax credits

CREDIT	$ AMOUNT
Child tax credit	
Additional child tax credit	
Earned income credit	
American opportunity credit	
Other expected tax credits	
TOTAL TAX CREDITS (ADD THESE UP AND ENTER AS A NEGATIVE)	$

Step 9: Enter the total income tax payments you've already made

PAYMENT TYPE	$ AMOUNT
Federal income taxes withheld from paychecks (use the YTD number)	
Federal income taxes withheld from retirement distributions	
Other federal income taxes withheld	
Estimated payments already made	
Total federal income tax payments made (add these up and enter as a negative)	
ESTIMATED FEDERAL TAXES STILL DUE* =	$

*If you plan to make estimated tax payments, divide the total due by the number of remaining estimated tax payment dates. Record any estimated tax payments you make here.

ESTIMATED TAX PAYMENT DATES			
PAYMENT #	**PAYMENT DUE DATE**	**PAYMENTS MADE (ENTER THE DOLLAR AMOUNT OF YOUR PAYMENT AND THE DATE YOU SUBMITTED IT)**	
Payment 1	April 15	$	/ /
Payment 2	June 15	$	/ /
Payment 3	September 15	$	/ /
Payment 4	January 15 (of the next year)	$	/ /

Notes:

HOW MUCH SHOULD I BORROW?

✅ Use this worksheet to figure out how much money you need to borrow to carry you through the crisis period. Pull the amounts from the Ongoing Crisis Costs worksheet you completed in Chapter 2, as well as from the Short-Term Crisis Budget, Periodic Expenses Calendar, and Cash Resources worksheets you completed in Chapter 3.

UPCOMING EXPENSES	$ AMOUNT
Regular monthly expenses	
Number of months your income/income opportunities may be reduced	
Monthly expenses × number of months	
Periodic expenses	
Crisis expenses	
Other expenses	
Total Upcoming Expenses	$
CASH SOURCES	**$ AMOUNT**
Reliable/guaranteed monthly income	
Monthly income × number of months your income/income opportunities may be reduced	
Non-retirement cash resources	
Retirement account loans or withdrawals	
Total Cash Available to Cover Expenses	$

CASH COVERAGE NEEDS (SUBTRACT CASH AVAILABLE TO COVER FROM TOTAL UPCOMING EXPENSES)	$
Extra coverage factor (10% or 20%)	
Extra coverage (total upcoming expenses × the extra coverage factor you chose)	
Amount to Borrow	$

PLANNED PAYBACK STRATEGY	
When you'll be able to start repaying	
Affordable monthly payment	$
Expected time line to pay off loan (in months or years)	

Notes:

RESOURCES FOR AID CHECKLIST

✔️ Use this worksheet to keep a log of the aid you've applied for. Following a request, you'll probably need to follow up. You'll find a list of possible resources at https://michelecagancpa.com/FinRec101.

ORGANIZATION	TYPE OF ASSISTANCE

Notes:

FIRST CONTACT DATE	FOLLOW UP	AID RECEIVED

CHAPTER FIVE

REDUCING MONEY GOING OUT

Making some *temporary* expense cuts can free up more space in your budget than you may realize. At first this can seem impossible, but as you start taking a closer look at your monthly spending, you'll find a lot of areas where you can start shrinking your expenses. The key here is perspective. If you look at this as "tightening your belt" or "pinching pennies," it turns into a chore you'll want to avoid. But if you turn that outlook around and think of it as more of a treasure hunt, looking for ways to free up money can feel fulfilling—even fun (honestly!). At the very least, you'll feel a sense of relief as you reduce the amount of money leaving your bank account every month.

Plus, reducing your cash outflow doesn't rely completely on cutting expenses. It also involves delaying or reducing as many of your monthly payments as you can. And, in some cases, it means putting regular monthly expenses on your credit cards instead of using up precious cash resources. Your journey to freeing up cash begins in the following chapter, with discovering new ways to downsize even essential expenses and identifying unnecessary spending—meaning money going toward things you don't even want. You'll also find some cash boosting strategies here that focus on changing the timing of expenses, working with creditors to reduce or suspend payments, strategically turning to credit cards. Use a combination strategy here to minimize both your current financial stress and your long-term financial problems. If you're stuck with a choice between surviving today and denting your financial future, focus on today first...and we'll fix that future dent in the future.

Downsize Any Expenses You Can

Trimming down your budget is a critical part of managing your cash flow right now. You may need to make some deep cuts here, but the key is in *strategic* cuts that serve your financial situation rather than just randomly slashing spending.

In this situation, where current cash flow ranks as your number one priority, downsizing expenses doesn't mean living by candle-light or eating cold cereal out of the box. You don't have to cut out lattes if they're the only bright spot in your day. This cutback is not about your long-term budget. It's about freeing up cash flow for your crisis budget. That means getting rid of expenses that don't serve you right now, shrinking some other expenses, and delaying any payments that you can.

Weirdly, it can be easier to reduce a few large expenses—and essential expenses often take up a big chunk of the budget—than to try to lower dozens of smaller expenses. And that's what we're going for here: the quickest, easiest way to make sure you can afford to pay for your essential expenses during this situation.

CUTTING COSTS THAT DON'T SERVE YOU

When money isn't an issue, or at least not a dire issue, it's easy to fall into overspending patterns without even realizing it. That doesn't necessarily mean spending more money than you have. Rather, it means spending money on things that you don't actually want.

To be clear, you may think you want whatever it is when you're buying it. But many people—myself included—sometimes buy things on impulse or out of boredom or other emotion that we end up never using. And it's not just tangible things, like clothes or exercise equip-ment; it's also memberships, courses, subscriptions, and other ser-vices that you set up on autopay. Those recurring costs can do even more damage than impulse buys because they're completely passive spending. In fact, you may not even realize that you're still spending that money. Use the Hidden Expenses Checklist at the end of this chapter to uncover expenses that have gone unnoticed.

TEMPORARY BUDGET CUTS

Cutting costs for things you don't *need* right now—but absolutely want—can free up room in your budget. Then, once your cash flow is in better shape, you can add them back in. These types of expenses include a combination of things you can't do right now but would want to get back to at some point, or things that you do really want but that don't make the essentials list. Examples of expenses that can be temporarily cut include:

- Housekeeping
- Car wash
- Dog grooming
- Personal services (like manicures and haircuts)
- Recreational activities
- Dining out
- Landscaping/yard work
- Kids' activities (sports, music lessons, camps)
- Paid streaming services

Use the Expenses to Cut worksheet at the end of this chapter to identify these expenses and see how much cash you'll be freeing up.

Pause Recurring Donations

When every dime matters to your financial well-being, it's okay to stop your recurring charitable contributions. You originally set these up to spread your donations over the course of the year. Now, your monthly cash flow can't support that. So pause the auto-contributions, and as soon as you're able to, you can donate the full amount you would have given.

Every dollar normally spent on these wants can go straight toward your essential expenses. If your essentials are covered right now without making any of these cuts, cut these expenses anyway—for now—and put the money you're not spending on them straight into your emergency savings. Once your crisis has passed, and you're back on secure financial footing, you can add any or all of these back into your budget. And by proactively trimming them, you might be able to add them back much sooner than you'd expect.

TIMING MATTERS

When you're experiencing a cash crunch, cash flow timing really matters. Wherever possible, try to reset the due dates for bills to sync up with when you typically receive cash (from whatever sources). The easiest way to do this is with the Paying Monthly Bills Calendar worksheet at the end of this chapter. Go through all of your bills and mark the due dates on this worksheet. If you pay online, you have more control over when payments will hit your bank account. If you write checks and mail them, you'll need to give yourself a five-day cushion to make sure payments arrive by their due dates, so note that on the calendar as well.

Once all the bills are mapped out, mark your *reliable* incoming cash flows on the calendar. Hopefully, these will arrive right before your priority expense payments are due. If not, you can ask your creditors to change your due date. In fact, you can often do that yourself if you have online access to your account. It can take a month or two to kick in, so do this as soon as you can. You'll find it easier to manage paying bills when the timing matches better.

Minimize Essential Expenses

You can't completely cut out essential expenses: They're the basics you need to survive. But you *can* reduce or defer them, at least temporarily. You can use a combination of pruning and pausing strategies to deal with these essentials until the immediate cash crisis has passed.

Some of these solutions will make long-term changes to your monthly expenses, things like refinancing your mortgage or getting rid of a high-cost car. Most, though, are short-term bridge solutions that can stay in place until you don't need them anymore. And all of them can make it easier to stretch out your cash and avoid (or at least minimize) additional debt.

HOUSING

The best way to lower your housing costs is to move to a less expensive home. If that option is available to you and you can handle the stress of moving on top of everything else, it can make a huge difference to your financial situation. This strategy works better for renters than homeowners but can work for motivated sellers with in-demand homes.

Moving isn't your only option for cost-cutting here, though. It might seem nearly impossible to reduce your housing costs without moving, but there are some other things you can try, such as:

- Refinancing your mortgage if you have decent credit and can get a lower interest rate
- Asking your lender to lower your rate if your mortgage is in good standing (you'll be surprised how often they say yes)
- Checking into property tax relief, which many states offer through either rebates or tax credits

- Negotiating a rental reduction—even a temporary one—with your landlord by offering to sign a longer-term lease or switching to biweekly (rather than monthly) payments
- Doing your own—or postponing—household cleaning, simple home repairs and maintenance, and yard work, rather than hiring out

You can also try another approach: If it makes sense to your situation, get a roommate or boarder to help offset a portion of your rent or mortgage payments, and possibly also utility payments. Keep in mind that this could possibly affect your income taxes, so talk to your tax preparer to find out if you need to take any proactive steps to minimize a potential tax issue.

GAS AND ELECTRIC

Skipping payments on your gas and electric bill can leave you without power—no lights, no heat, no refrigerator. Even if you're not yet in a situation where you can't manage these bills, you should contact your utility company as soon as your circumstances have changed. You'll want to apply for emergency assistance before you've missed one or more payments, and before you're in danger of having your utilities disconnected.

You may also be able to reduce your energy bills by:

- Weatherizing your home and making it more energy-efficient with simple touches like weather-stripping your windows and sealing small holes and gaps
- Installing a smart thermostat
- Replacing your furnace or A/C filter regularly
- Checking if your utility company has lower rates for off-peak use, and doing things like laundry during those hours

Taking steps like these can drastically reduce your energy spending, especially if you live somewhere that gets brutally cold or unbearably hot. You can also check to see whether your utility offers budget billing (they may call it something else), where you pay the same amount every month regardless of actual usage so at least you're never hit with enormous surprise bills.

FOOD

Groceries can eat up a big chunk of your monthly cash flow. Luckily, there are simple ways to save on food without changing your family's regular eating habits. Strategies that will help reduce your grocery bill include:

- Making a meal plan for the week
- Grocery shopping once a week with a list—and sticking to the list
- Buying nonperishable foods like cereal, pasta, and rice in bulk rather than the more expensive prepackaged versions
- Avoiding or limiting buying prepared foods
- Having "clean out the pantry" days where you use up staples before buying more food
- Using cash (rather than debit or credit cards) whenever possible to pay for groceries, which will help you stick to your list and dodge impulse purchases
- Ordering online and doing curbside pickup rather than going into the store to do your shopping
- Using apps like Ibotta, BerryCart, and Rakuten that offer rebates or cash back for your regular purchases

And though it will save you money on groceries over the long haul, *don't stock up*. Right now, cash flow is more important than anything. So, while stocking up on sale items makes sense for a regular household budget, it's a bad idea for a crisis budget. That said, you still want to be aware of sales before you shop whenever possible. That way you can time some regular, currently necessary grocery purchases to coincide with sales.

MEDICINE AND MEDICAL CARE

Medical bills can be extremely frustrating, as they're virtually impossible to plan. You often won't know how much you're being charged for any service or how much insurance might—or might not—cover until after the fact. And, of course, you don't want to skimp on medical care, but you may be able to reduce some costs or postpone some nonurgent appointments (like routine dental checkups) during your cash crunch.

When you receive any medical bill, review it quickly and completely. Medical bills may be full of mistakes, such as including procedures you didn't have. Small things like incorrect diagnosis codes can lead to automatic rejection from your insurance company. So before you add any medical bill into your budget or send any payment, make sure the charges are correct and that the correct information was sent to your insurance. If your insurance company rejects a bill, ask them why or appeal the decision. Many appeals result in insurance coverage for a previously rejected claim.

On top of verifying your medical bills and coverage, you can also take steps to reduce your out-of-pocket costs. Here are some possibilities for saving money without skipping medical care:

- Use in-network providers when you can
- Ask your doctor for generic prescriptions rather than name-brand drugs
- Use online or mail-order pharmacies for long-term medications (just make sure to check with your healthcare provider or insurance company to verify that they're legitimate)
- Look into drug assistance programs such as NeedyMeds (www.needymeds.org)
- Use apps like GoodRx to find the lowest prescription drug prices in your area

These options may not work for everyone. Your preferred providers may all be out of network, for example, or generic alternatives may not work as effectively for you as brand-name drugs. If you can't reduce your medical costs outright, talk with your providers and let them know you're having temporary cash flow problems. Many of them will let you defer payments or set up payment plans to ease the financial burden on your family.

TRANSPORTATION

Cars (that you own) are budget hogs, even when they're completely paid off. They come with plenty of ongoing expenses attached, from annual registration fees to gas to insurance to regular maintenance (like oil changes). Those costs alone can put a pretty big hole in your budget, and they don't even include repairs for when something breaks down—usually at the absolute worst time. Still, you probably need your car to get to work, school, or medical appointments. So, while you may not be able to erase those expenses, you can shrink some of them.

If you have a large, new, or high-cost vehicle, consider trading it in for a small, economical alternative—preferably used. Smaller cars, for example, cost much less to own and operate than larger cars or SUVs. You can save money on gas by using apps like GasBuddy to find the lowest local prices. And you'll find ways to slash your car insurance bill a little later in this chapter.

> ### Is It Worth Almost $10,000 a Year?
> According to the AAA's "Your Driving Costs" report, the average cost to own a car in 2020 was $9,561. That included an average $1,200 in annual insurance costs and $851 in registration, taxes, and licenses. Small sedans clocked in as the lowest-cost vehicles, at an average 50.1 cents per mile compared to large sedans at 74.55 cents, medium SUVs at 66.91 cents, and minivans at 67.34 cents.

If you live in an area where you can get by without a car, you can save a lot of money by selling it and using alternative transportation. And for times when you really do need a car rather than public transportation, there are several ride-sharing options you can use, such as:

- Zipcar, a membership-based car-sharing company that gives you access to cars whenever you need them
- Ride shares like Uber and Lyft
- Rental car companies like Budget and Enterprise

Even though it feels expensive, using these options occasionally costs much less than owning and maintaining your own vehicle.

SAVING MONEY IS NOT THE ONLY FACTOR

It might seem like downsizing essential expenses involves purely financial decisions, but it's important to also take your life into account. For example, cutting takeout meals or prepared foods from your budget might seem like a no-brainer. But if you're working two jobs, taking care of your family, and dealing with the stress of a financial crisis, takeout might be a much better budget choice than ingredients that require time, effort, and energy that you just can't spare. So, keeping with this example, if prepared food makes sense for your life, make it a line item in your budget, but put a hard limit on the spending.

Before you put an expense on the chopping block, think about the impact on your life as well as the financial effect. If it's truly something that you need, even if it's not technically an essential expense, find a responsible way to work it into your crisis budget. If it starts draining too much cash flow, add extra limits. For example, reduce takeout dinners from five times a week to three times, or stick with lower-cost prepared foods.

Even during this temporary crisis, you need to have a plan you can live with and stick to, or you won't be able to follow it. Your plan has some flexibility, so as long as you're careful about this "nonessential but essential for you" spending, you'll be able to make this work.

AVOIDING UNNECESSARY CHARGES

Along with cutting back and delaying expenses, another key part of your plan to minimize these costs involves avoiding unnecessary charges such as:

- Late payment penalties
- Underpayment penalties
- Penalty interest rates on credit cards
- Over-limit penalties on credit cards
- Bank fees for things like bounced checks or foreign ATMs
- IRS fees for failure to file, late filing, or late payments

Avoiding some of these penalties may call for communication with whatever company you're dealing with (more on how to do that in the next section). Others fall solidly within your control. For example, if you can pay a bill, make sure you pay it on time. If your bank charges fees when your balance drops below a certain amount, maintain that minimum balance or change to a no-fee account. Don't write checks that you know—or even think—might bounce. And even if you can't afford to pay your income tax bill in full, make sure to file your tax return on time to at least avoid late filing penalties.

FINDING THE LOWEST PRICES ON EVERYDAY NEEDS

When you don't have tons of time to shop around, you may end up paying more for things than you need to. But even with limited time and energy, you can take advantage of these tools to help you find the best prices on essentials with minimal effort.

To save money on everyday purchases, consider using:

- Browser extensions like Honey that actively seek out lower prices and coupon codes as you shop online
- Price comparison websites like *PriceGrabber* and *Google Shopping*
- Apps like ShopSavvy or BuyVia that let you scan items as you shop to let you know where you can get them locally for less

These savings boosters painlessly chip away at your spending. And while you probably won't save thousands of dollars, they will help free up space in a tight budget.

Don't Ditch Insurance— Minimize Your Premiums

As you're going through your list of expenses, you might be thinking about getting rid of insurance. After all, it's usually one of the biggest line items in every budget. Canceling insurance to save money is a very common mistake, and one you really want to avoid. Your financial situation is already under stress, so you don't want to toss the safety nets you already have in place that can help minimize the cost of other crises.

That said, you absolutely can cut out the fat in any of your policies and reduce coverage everywhere that makes sense. If your policies aren't already bundled, meaning you have multiple policies with a single insurer, look into how moving toward that might save you money without cutting coverage. You can also do some cost-comparison shopping online, especially if you've been using the same insurance company for a long time (because that's easier than switching).

Set aside some time to look over all of your different insurance policies and figure out how much you're paying for each type of coverage. That should be spelled out in the first few pages of the policy or on your annual policy bill. Most major insurance companies also let you look at and change your coverage online.

Before you make coverage changes, you'll want to check in with your state laws (such as for car insurance) or loan agreements (such as for homeowners insurance when you have an outstanding mortgage). You may be obligated to maintain specific coverage levels to meet those requirements. The important thing to remember here is this: Don't cut coverage that you truly need— only coverage that you can *temporarily* do without.

CAR INSURANCE

Almost every state has minimum requirements for car insurance, and you can find that information on your state insurance commissioner's website. Even if you normally carry higher coverage levels, right now you'll want to pare your policy down to the bone to preserve cash. Your first move: Increase your deductibles—that's the fastest, easiest way to lower your premiums.

Next, take a look at the types of coverage your policy contains. Most insurers offer six types of coverage:

1. **Liability:** pays out if you cause an accident that harms other people or property.
2. **Personal injury protection (PIP):** covers medical expenses for you and the other passengers in your car no matter who caused the accident.

PIP May Offer More

In addition to covering medical expenses, some PIP policies also cover things like lost wages and childcare costs related to the accident. These policies normally pay out for these expenses right away as soon as you've met the deductible.

---

3. **Uninsured/underinsured motorist:** pays out for your medical expenses in an accident caused by another driver with inadequate insurance.
4. **Collision:** covers damage to your car caused by an accident no matter who was at fault.
5. **Comprehensive:** covers repairs or replacement for your car for anything other than an accident, such as a fallen tree branch or vandalism.
6. **Gap:** covers the difference between your car's current value and the amount you owe on a loan or lease.

Some of these are required by state law or lenders, but others—like comprehensive coverage—are optional.

If you have higher than minimum coverage or coverage that isn't required, consider your reasons for choosing those options and decide what you can do without during your crisis. You can always add coverage back once your budget has room for that.

HEALTH INSURANCE

Health insurance can be tricky to reduce, because most options are available only during open enrollment periods. If you have health insurance through your employer and need assistance with your portion of premium payments, contact your HR department immediately to see what kind of assistance they may offer.

If you have health insurance through your state's Health Insurance Marketplace, you may be able to make changes to your plan based on specific life events, including:

- Losing job-based coverage
- Getting divorced
- Having a child
- Having a reduced household income

The key here is to make sure that the health insurance plan you choose connects to how you and your family use medical care, especially when your main goal is to lower your monthly cash drain. A high-deductible health plan with a super-low premium will save you money on insurance, but if anyone in your family needs regular medical care, you could end up paying more out of pocket than if you had a plan with more coverage. Make sure to look at the combination of insurance premiums and your regular medical expenses before you choose a policy. If you can't afford health insurance premiums right now, you can look into Medicaid or the Children's Health Insurance Program (CHIP), both of which offer no- or low-cost health coverage for people and families in need.

HOMEOWNERS/RENTERS INSURANCE

Homeowners insurance costs can vary by hundreds of dollars per month, depending on a variety of factors. While you don't want to completely cut this crucial insurance, you may be able to significantly reduce your premiums by making targeted changes.

First, look at your deductible. The standard for homeowners insurance is $500, but you may be able to increase your deductible to as much as $2,500. That change can dramatically lower your premiums, and you don't have to stop there. You'll also want to take another look at your policy to see exactly what's covered. For example, insurance companies price policies based on the value of your house, which often includes the land your house is on. But the land isn't subject to the same kind of damage as your house (it can't burn down, for example), so it shouldn't necessarily be included in the value quoted on your policy.

Can I Ditch My PMI?

Private mortgage insurance (PMI) gets automatically tacked on to your mortgage payment with down payments of less than 20 percent. Mortgage lenders have to cancel the PMI once your equity in the home hits 78 percent, but you may be able to ditch this extra expense sooner. When your mortgage balance drops to 80 percent of your home's original value, send a written request to your lender to cancel the PMI—and they have to do so, as long as you have a good payment history.

Next, you'll want to make sure that your policy contains every discount you're eligible for. For example, many insurance companies offer discounts for home security measures, such as alarms, smoke detectors, and deadbolt locks. Some companies offer discounts to adults older than fifty-five, people with excellent credit scores, and customers who've been enrolled for at least five years (called longevity discounts). These credits can add up and take another slice off of your homeowners insurance premiums.

If you have renters insurance—and most people don't, though it's good to have—you may be able to lower your premiums by:

- Checking to see if you're eligible for any group or member discounts
- Increasing your deductible
- Reporting any safety features, such as alarms, deadbolts, and fire extinguishers
- Asking your landlord to make safety upgrades, such as installing deadbolts, which will lower their premiums as well

Taking these steps can help reduce your outgoing cash without stripping away the insurance protection you count on.

LIFE INSURANCE

A lot of people consider canceling their life insurance when they hit a financial rough patch, but you'll want to keep yours if at all possible. How to handle this depends on whether you have term or permanent (also called whole) life insurance.

Permanent policies come with more options than term insurance when you're having cash flow struggles. With these policies, you may be able to:

- Use existing cash value inside the policy to pay your premiums
- Use dividends (if your policy pays them) to offset the cost of premiums
- Decrease the death benefit (if your insurance company allows that)

You may also want to consider cashing out your permanent life insurance policy (less any cancellation fees), and using the funds to beef up your emergency savings, pay some urgent bills, or switch to a term life insurance policy.

When it comes to reducing term life insurance premiums, there's really only one option: reducing the death benefit. Most insurers will allow you to change your coverage at least once while you hold the policy. Some allow multiple changes, so you could reduce your coverage now and increase it when your financial situation stabilizes. Lowering the face value of the policy can let you substantially reduce your annual premiums, and still offer your family at least some protection.

WHERE TO FIND HELP NAVIGATING INSURANCE OPTIONS

The easiest way to navigate your own insurance options is to enlist a licensed professional independent insurance agent. Some of them specialize in one type of policy, like health insurance, while others have broader expertise, like all types of personal (as opposed to business) policies. These independent insurance professionals don't work for a single insurance company. Rather, they're experts who know the ins and outs of dozens of policies from dozens of insurers, so they can help you find the best possible policy for you based on your insurance needs and budget limits. Best of all for your budget, you don't pay the insurance professional—they get paid by the insurance company you choose.

Take It from a CPA

I worked with a health insurance broker to help me sort through the best options for my family, which includes a child with chronic health problems. As it turned out, if I'd gotten the cheapest policy (which I totally intended to do), I would have ended up paying out much more money overall. Because we use a lot of ongoing medical care, a policy with higher premiums actually ended up saving us money during the year.

Along with helping you find the best policies for your family's needs, independent agents can also give you a heads-up when your insurance company plans to increase rates. They may also be able to help you file claims and communicate with your insurance company. You can find information about choosing an independent insurance agent on the National Association of Insurance Commissioners (NAIC) website at www.naic.org.

Work with Your Creditors

Here's the number one thing you need to know about your creditors (the people and companies you owe money to): They want to get paid. They don't want to take you to court. They don't want to send you to collections. They just want you to send them money.

When you can't pay your bills, calling your creditors jumps to the top of your to-do list. As long as you contact them before you miss a payment, they—at least most of them—will work with you. Why? See the previous paragraph.

There are a few ways creditors can offer assistance when you're having a money crunch, including:

- Making your payments smaller
- Letting you pay only interest for a while
- Temporarily pausing your payments altogether

None of these let you off the hook for the full amount you owe. In fact, using any of these methods will increase the amount you owe overall. Right now, though, that doesn't matter as much as getting some much-needed temporary financial relief. And once your finances have stabilized, you'll be able to quickly catch up and pay down your debt.

Your options depend on the types and amount of debt you're dealing with, along with your past payment history and current financial situation. You can get ahead of potential problems by applying for any of these options that you qualify for before any of your debt goes into default (nonpayment) status. As you begin to work with your creditors, use the Working with Creditors Log at the end of this chapter to capture the details of each communication.

STUDENT LOANS

If you have federal student loans, you'll find that there are several ways to reduce or defer payments without defaulting. The federal government offers payment plans based on your current income as well as the opportunity to put your loans on pause for one to three years.

Your first step here is to call your loan *servicer* as soon as you know you won't be able to make a full payment on time. With federal student loans, it's possible—even likely—that you'll have more than one loan servicer to deal with. You can find out which companies service your loans by logging in to your Federal Student Aid (FSA) account. Once you contact them, they'll be able to help you figure out whether you'll be better off with a modified payment plan or a temporary loan deferral.

If you decide to pause your loan payments, you can apply for loan deferment or forbearance. The two main differences here involve how long the program lasts and how interest gets treated while you're not making payments. In most cases, the interest portion of your paused payments will be added to your loan balance every month, meaning you'll end up owing more than you borrowed. But if you have *subsidized loans* or *Perkins Loans* (which you can also find out in your FSA account), the government will pick up the tab for that interest while your loan is in *deferment*.

Loan deferments of up to three years are available for people facing economic hardships who qualify. You have to request a deferral from your loan servicer, and if you meet the eligibility requirements, they have to grant it. You may be eligible for deferment if you're:

- Unemployed
- Earning income that's less than 150 percent of your state's poverty level
- Active duty military
- In the Peace Corps
- Getting treated for cancer
- Attending school half time or more
- Receiving federal or state assistance (such as SNAP)

If you don't qualify for deferment, you may still be able to get loan forbearance of up to one year from your servicer. The decision is usually up to them, but there are some circumstances where they have to grant it. Mandatory forbearance situations require that you have a federal direct student loan and that one of the following applies:

- You're currently serving in an AmeriCorps position
- You're in the middle of a medical or dental internship or residency
- You're an activated National Guard member
- The total monthly payments on all of your federal student loans is more than 20 percent of your monthly gross income

If none of those situations apply to you, you may still be able to get general forbearance if your lender approves it. You can qualify for general forbearance if you lose your job, experience financial problems, have high medical expenses, or any other reason your loan servicer allows.

While deferment and forbearance may seem like your best options, they may not be. If you can afford to make any payments at all, your overall long-term financial situation will be better served by choosing a downsized repayment plan. Federal student loan payment plans that are based on your current income and can help free up space in your crisis budget include:

- **Pay As You Earn (PAYE):** payments equal 10 percent of your discretionary income but are never more than you'd pay on the standard plan (the default ten-year plan), for up to twenty years.
- **Revised Pay As You Earn (REPAYE):** payments equal 10 percent of your discretionary income with no payment cap, for up to twenty or twenty-five years (depending on whether the loans were for undergrad or graduate school).
- **Income-Based Repayment (IBR):** payments equal either 10 or 15 percent of your discretionary income (depending on whether you took out the loans before or after July 1, 2014) but are never more than the standard plan payments, for up to twenty-five years.
- **Income-Contingent Repayment (ICR):** payments equal 20 percent of your discretionary income for up to twenty-five years.

Each of these payment options requires that you certify your income and your family size every year. As your discretionary income increases, so will your payments (unless they hit the standard payment cap). If you don't recertify on time, your payments will automatically increase, usually back to the standard plan payment.

Keep in mind that with income-driven repayment plans, your new monthly payment may not be enough to cover the monthly interest charge. That unpaid interest will be added to your loan balance. But as soon as your finances rebound, you can go back to making full payments—or even extra payments.

What If I Have Private Student Loans?

Private loans don't offer the same options when you're facing a financial challenge. You can contact your servicer to see if they'll provide any kind of assistance, such as *SoFi*'s Unemployment Protection Program or Sallie Mae's forbearance option. If such options are not available to you, look into refinancing your student loans at a lower interest rate or over a longer term to reduce monthly payments.

You can find complete information about managing your federal student loans, the qualifications for each payment plan, and a "Loan Simulator" tool that can help you test out different options on the Federal Student Aid website at www.studentaid.gov.

MORTGAGE LOANS

When you can't afford to pay your mortgage, your first call will be to your mortgage servicer, which may not be the same company that originally loaned you the money to buy your house. You can find the contact information for your mortgage servicer, the company you make payment to, on your monthly statement or online. When you get in touch, let them know that you can't make your payment and why.

They'll probably ask you a bunch of questions, so be prepared to answer things like:

- Whether the situation is temporary or permanent
- Details about the changes in your income and expenses
- Information about other resources, like savings and investments
- Whether you plan to stay in the home for at least one year
- How much you can afford to pay monthly right now (even if that's nothing)

You may have to complete an application for mortgage assistance that will help them figure out which options could be available for you. Options may include:

- Refinancing your mortgage loan, which replaces the old loan with a new one and can lower your monthly payments by adding time to your mortgage term, lowering your interest rate, or both
- A loan modification, which changes the terms of your loan (without refinancing) by extending the loan term, reducing the interest rate, or changing the type of loan (for example, switching from adjustable to fixed rate)
- Forbearance, which allows you to dramatically reduce or temporarily stop making mortgage payments for a specific period, then requires those missed payments to be paid back either in one lump sum or over a period of time

Remember, your mortgage servicer would rather work with you than have to deal with all of the hassles of foreclosure. So listen to the options they suggest and figure out which makes the most sense for you.

See the Full Picture

Be aware that some options for assistance can come with sizable drawbacks, such as a drop in your credit score, an income tax bill, loan fees and expenses (such as closing costs), or thousands of dollars in extra interest over the life of your loan. Make sure you understand both the immediate and long-term effects before choosing an option to reduce your mortgage payments.

Once you've settled on a plan, make sure you stick with it or notify your loan servicer immediately if you can't.

MEDICAL DEBT

In some ways, it's easier to deal with medical debt than other types of debt. Most service providers, such as doctors or hospitals, will negotiate with you as long as you reach out to them. In some cases, you may be able to reduce the amount of the bill, especially if there's an outrageous charge included (like $250 for a single dose of Tylenol). And if you can't get the amount due reduced, you can almost always set up a reasonable payment plan as long as your bill has not already been sent to collections.

Contact your service provider as soon as you can to get a payment plan set up. In many cases, as long as you make your scheduled payments on time, there won't be any interest charged on the medical debt. Stay in touch with your provider and let them know ahead of time if you won't be able to make a payment, and when you plan to make it up. Staying in contact with them will help keep your bill out of collections, which keeps it from damaging your credit score.

Another option: Take advantage of your healthcare provider's in-house financing program. Many providers offer this option, and it can be helpful when your budget is tight. Be aware that these plans usually come with fairly high interest rates—often higher than the rates for personal loans—but they offer long payback periods that minimize monthly payments. Before signing on for this type of financing, make sure that you won't face any penalties for prepayments, because you'll want to pay off this high-rate debt as soon as you're able to.

CREDIT CARD DEBT

If you can't swing even your minimum credit card payments during your financial crisis, contact all of your credit card companies immediately. Depending on how long you expect to need assistance, they may offer you a variety of options from allowing one skipped payment to temporarily reducing minimum payments to enrolling you in a hardship program. The options available depend on your credit card company, your payment history with that company, and your budget. The sooner you make contact—preferably before you've missed a single payment—the more leeway most credit card companies will offer. Keep in mind, though, that these plans benefit them more than you in the long run, as you will end up paying a lot of extra interest while your credit card debt remains on the books.

Credit card hardship programs (sometimes called payment assistance or financial relief programs) work sort of like payment plans for your credit card debt. You may qualify for one of these programs if you've experienced a major life change such as a job loss, a serious illness, a divorce, or a natural disaster. During the plan, your credit card company may help out by lowering your interest rate—sometimes to 0 percent—or waiving some fees. Be aware that reduced payments may not cover the full amount of monthly interest due, which means that a portion of that interest may be added to your credit card balance. The company may also reduce your credit limit, freeze your card for spending, or even cancel the card, so make sure you fully understand the terms of your deal.

Credit card companies that offer some type of hardship programs include:

- Discover
- American Express
- Bank of America
- Capital One

Each company has a different process for enrolling you in its hardship program, but the basics are all the same:

- Step 1: Before you apply, look at your crisis budget and figure out how much you can reliably pay each month.
- Step 2: Contact your credit card issuer by phone, using the number associated with that company's hardship program. If you call the regular customer service number, tell them immediately that you've had a financial hardship.
- Step 3: When you reach the right representative, be up front about your situation and honest about your budget.
- Step 4: Take detailed notes during the conversation (or record the call if you can).
- Step 5: Repeat the terms back to the representative to make sure you understand everything correctly.
- Step 6: Do not enter into an agreement during the initial call. Ask the representative how you can get back in touch to finalize the agreement.
- Step 7: Take some time to figure out how and whether their offer will work within your crisis budget.
- Step 8: Call them back whether or not you decide to enroll in their hardship program. If you do, be prepared to prove your hardship with backup documentation.

Some of these programs may require you to meet with a credit counselor or take a debt management course. The agreement may also require that you set up automatic payments from your bank account. If that's a requirement, make sure that your account has enough money on the withdrawal day in order to avoid having the agreement canceled and getting hit with fees and penalties from both the credit card company and your bank.

> ## Money-Saving Tip:
> ## Make Multiple Small Payments Every Month
>
> Credit card companies charge interest based on your average monthly balance. You can reduce that number by making several small payments throughout the month rather than one big payment on the due date. By paying a portion of your planned payment early in the cycle, you'll be reducing your average monthly balance. A lower average monthly balance means less interest will be charged. This strategy has the *triple benefit* of paying down your credit card debt faster, minimizing your interest charges, and stretching out your available cash.

Hardship programs can help ease your cash flow burdens during your financial crisis. And while they will temporarily hurt your net worth, you can fix that once this cash crunch has passed and you're able to begin aggressively paying down debt.

INCOME TAX DEBT

If you owe money to the IRS but can't afford to make full payments right now, you can work out a plan with them to avoid getting hit with big penalties and tax liens. How you'll approach the situation depends on whether this is a new tax debt that you won't be able to pay on time or you're having trouble with an existing IRS payment plan.

The IRS offers a few different payment plan options, so you'll be able to find one that fits your situation. In most cases, you'll be able to complete and submit your application online, but you can also do this by regular mail or in person at your local IRS office if you prefer.

If This Is a New Tax Debt

If you owe taxes when you file your current tax return but just can't afford to pay the bill on time, don't worry: you have a lot of options. And most of them are very easy to set up and deal with. The most important thing to remember here is to file your taxes on time anyway, so you won't get hit with late filing penalties on top of everything else.

The IRS offers both short-term and long-term payment plans. Here's how they work: With short-term plans, you'll agree to pay the full amount you owe within 120 days. These plans have no setup fees, but the IRS will charge interest until your balance has been paid in full. Their long-term payment plans, also called installment agreements, are available when you don't think you'll be able to pay off your tax debt within 120 days. You'll have two options for setting up your long-term payment plan:

1. Direct Debit Installment Agreement (DDIA), where the IRS will automatically pull the monthly payment from your bank account. This option comes with a $31 setup fee if you apply online.

2. You initiate the monthly payment, using either Direct Pay (their ACH option), online payments, checks, money orders, or debit or credit cards (which come with an additional fee). This option charges a $149 setup fee if you apply online.

You can find full details for both types of plans and online applications on the IRS website at www.irs.gov.

If You Already Have a Payment Plan

When you already have a payment plan with the IRS, it's best to take immediate action, before you're late with even a single payment. And if you have missed a payment, try to get in touch with the IRS as soon as you are able. Your first move here will be to review your payment. You can look at the details of your personal plan by going to the IRS website (www.irs.gov) and logging in to their "Online Payment Agreement" tool. If you can't access your plan online for any reason, call the IRS at 1-800-829-1040.

Once you are logged in, you can view your plan and make changes to it, including:

- Changing your monthly due date
- Changing your monthly payment
- Changing your payment method to DDIA
- Reinstating your payment plan after you've defaulted (missed a payment)

If the IRS tool doesn't like any of your changes—the payment amount is too small, for example—it will give you a chance to revise your changes. Be aware that if you need to reinstate your plan, the IRS may charge you a fee.

What about State Taxes?

The options available for state income tax payment plans vary from state to state, just like you'd expect. You can find the options, requirements, and applications on your state's income tax website, usually called the Department of Revenue or the Office of Tax and Revenue. Most states offer some form of payment plan, similar to the IRS installment agreements. You can also talk with your tax preparer to see if they're familiar with state and local tax payment plans, and discuss how to choose the best option for your situation.

Use Credit Cards for Essential Expenses When Absolutely Necessary

Under normal financial circumstances, you wouldn't want to use credit cards for essential expenses unless you knew you could and would pay the bills in full every month. Now, you want to carefully map out how and when you'll use your credit cards for three important reasons:

1. You don't want to build up debt that will be tough to manage once things go back to normal.
2. You don't want to pay double or triple for everything due to the added interest expense.
3. You don't want to use up all of your available credit in case another emergency—like a flat tire or a busted hot water heater—occurs.

That said, your credit cards provide a valuable resource when you're crunched for cash. And as with all of your other resources, you don't want to run through this one too quickly or without a clear plan.

HOW TO WEAVE CREDIT CARD USE INTO YOUR CRISIS BUDGET

Using credit cards to stretch cash flow can help your monthly cash last longer. At the same time, building up credit card debt can suck up more of your cash flow as minimum payments start increasing. The most effective strategy here is to use credit cards without creating unmanageable credit card debt. It may sound tricky, but all it takes is preplanning to make this work in your favor.

You'll have three main options here:

1. Using credit card points to pay expenses
2. Paying for expenses with your regular credit cards
3. Using credit cards still in the introductory rate phase

Working with a combination of these options can help you make ends meet during tight months. Before you start, create a plan that will help you avoid piling on credit card debt.

HOW TO PLAN YOUR CRISIS CREDIT CARD USAGE

The best way to minimize the potentially damaging impact of credit card spending involves creating and following a plan. You'll want to carefully consider things like interest rates, payment dates, and point systems to map out the most efficient, least harmful credit card strategy.

But the overall strategy will serve your full financial picture only if you don't double-spend the same money. Here's an example of what this means: When you use a credit card to buy groceries, count that money as spent on groceries in your budget even though you didn't put out any cash. If the amount that you spent doesn't get marked as spent, it might look like it's available to spend again.

The following sections will help you create your plan for using your credit card(s) during crisis.

Use Your Points

First, you'll want to use up all of your credit card points in a way that makes sense for your crisis budget. For example, if your credit card points program offers gift cards that pay for things like groceries and gas, get them. Some online sellers (like Amazon) let you use credit card points for purchases, and you can find many household essentials on those sites. If you can get cash back or a statement credit with your points, those options can also help make space in your budget.

> **Don't Lose Your Points!**
>
> You may be surprised to find out that you can lose credit card points that you've earned. The most common ways that this happens include making late payments, not using your credit card for more than three months, letting points expire, or declaring bankruptcy.

Using points doesn't cost you anything or add to your debt, making them a perfect first choice for credit card–related spending. Use the Credit Card Rewards Deals worksheet at the end of this chapter to inventory and track your points and keep up with all the deals your programs offer.

Using Existing Cards for Essentials

Think about your credit card sort of like an in-house payday loan here. You're using this financial space to cover essential expenses while you're waiting for your next incoming cash flow. Decide which expenses you'll put on the credit card in advance. Then look at which credit card makes the most sense to use for those expenses.

Start with your lowest-rate card just in case you end up being unable to pay off these charges right away. The exception here: Don't use a low-rate balance transfer card for new charges if you've already made a balance transfer. (More on this in the next section.)

If you know for sure that you'll be able to pay off these new charges by the next statement due date, look at the card that gives you the best rewards for that particular type of charge. For example, if one of your cards is running a 5 percent cash-back special for grocery and gas purchases, use that card instead of one that only offers 1 or 2 percent cash back. This strategy calls for knowing the current offers on all of your rewards cards. Use the

Credit Card Rewards Deals worksheet at the end of this chapter for updating all of the programs available to you.

Special Introductory Rate Cards

Next, look at the terms of any 0 percent or low-interest credit cards you have. If you've been using them for purchases, they go straight to the top of your list. Be mindful of the terms of your deal here, because the special rates will vanish if you make even the tiniest slipup. Here's what you need to know before you use these cards for essential expenses:

- When the introductory rate runs out
- If any type of use—such as cash advances—can invalidate the deal
- What happens if the full balance isn't paid off before the introductory rate ends
- Credit limit
- Minimum payment
- Payment due date

If you go over your credit limit or miss a payment due date, chances are you'll be hit with penalty fees and penalty interest rates, which may run as high as 29.99 percent.

If you've already used any of these cards to make balance transfers, put them on the bottom of your resource pile and try to avoid using them for purchases. When you add new charges to balance transfer cards, every payment you make goes toward the new purchases first. If there's any part of the original balance transfer left when the introductory period ends, you could end up with a very hefty pile of interest on top of your remaining balance due.

Be Prepared with a Payback Plan

If you're using credit cards as a way to manage your monthly cash flow—rather than because you don't have enough incoming cash to afford essentials—you can handle the cash in one of two ways:

1. Pay the current credit card expenses as soon as the money comes in
2. Put the money for those expenses aside and use it to pay your credit card bill by the due date

Either way, make sure that these new charges get paid right away so you don't end up in a more dire financial situation.

If you temporarily need to use credit cards to pay for some essential expenses because you couldn't otherwise afford them, keep close track of the charges and card balances. As the balances increase, so will the interest charges and minimum monthly payments. Make sure your crisis will be able to handle the higher monthly payments, or contact your credit card company immediately if you see that you can't. You'll also want to prevent accidentally going over your limit to avoid costly penalties. Remember, interest charges can push you over the limit, so keep a close eye on your balances—especially when your cards are getting close to maxed out.

Consider Whether Bankruptcy Is a Good Option

When you're experiencing a temporary financial setback, bank-ruptcy probably won't make much sense. After all, bankruptcy gets rid of existing debts but won't help you pay your regular bills if you can't cover those with your income.

But if your situation drags on, and your debt burden becomes unmanageable, filing for bankruptcy may be your best option. It really depends on your unique situation, based on your current and near-future financial facts. For most people, it's beneficial to work with a bankruptcy attorney, although the typical up-front cash outlay can make that tough when you're already having financial struggles.

The truth is that most people wait too long before declaring bankruptcy and end up doing much more damage to their long-term finances than if they'd filed sooner. That doesn't mean that anyone experiencing financial setbacks should immediately con-sider bankruptcy, though, because taking this action also comes with financial and emotional consequences.

Some factors that will play a big role in your decision include:

- Your home state
- The type of debt you have
- Your total debt in relation to your income
- The types of assets you own
- Whether you're currently in danger of losing money or pos-sessions to creditors
- Whether someone has cosigned for any of your debts

In addition to deciding *whether* to file for bankruptcy, you'll also have to figure out which *type* of bankruptcy makes the most sense in your situation. The two options for personal bankruptcy are Chapter 7 and Chapter 13. Both offer financial relief from debt but in very different ways, and both are covered later in this chapter.

PROS AND CONS OF BANKRUPTCY

Like most things, bankruptcy has both good and bad points to consider. In some situations, it's the smartest financial move you can make. But for others, it can be a horrible mistake.

The Pros:

- Collectors will stop hounding you
- You'll stop paying all of your bills *immediately*
- It gives you a chance to reboot your finances and financial habits
- You'll get some mandatory financial counseling
- Your credit score could rebound more quickly than if you continue to miss due dates
- Debts discharged through bankruptcy don't count as taxable income
- Creditors have to stop garnishing your wages and pulling money from your bank account

The Cons:

- Your credit score will take a hit
- The bankruptcy will stay on your credit report for seven to ten years
- You could lose all the credit card points and rewards you've earned
- Your bankruptcy will be recorded in public records
- It costs around $300–$350 in court fees to file
- Bankruptcy attorneys may charge $1,200–$4,000
- Bankruptcy does *not* eliminate all debts

Take the time to understand the effects filing bankruptcy will have on your current and future finances and look at both sides of the equation.

BANKRUPTCY TERMS YOU NEED TO KNOW

In order to understand how bankruptcy would work for you, you'll also need to understand the language. Here's a list of important bankruptcy vocabulary that you need to know:

- **Automatic stay:** an immediate halt to all collection efforts, including garnished wages and lawsuits, from every creditor.
- **Secured debt:** debts tied to specific assets that the creditor can take if you don't pay, such as foreclosing on a house when a mortgage goes unpaid.
- **Unsecured debt:** money you owe that is not tied to any kind of asset.
- **Exempt assets:** property and possessions, such as a house or a car, that the state allows you to keep after bankruptcy.
- **Cosigners:** people listed on your loan documents or accounts who are legally responsible for your debts if you don't pay them.
- **Liquidate:** when the courts sell or cash in your property and possessions to use as payment to creditors.
- **Claim:** a creditor's statement of their right to payment.
- **Discharge:** release from personal responsibility for debts.
- **Lien:** the right to take property as payment for a debt.

Getting familiar with these terms and ideas can help you figure out whether bankruptcy makes sense, and which form of bankruptcy would work better for your situation. Plus, it will make communicating with your bankruptcy attorney much easier and clearer.

CHAPTER 7

Chapter 7 bankruptcy is also known as liquidation or straight bankruptcy. It's used for people who can't make all of their debt payments with their income. To be eligible, your monthly income can't be more than the median monthly income in your state based on your family size. With Chapter 7, the court converts your assets (except for exempt assets) into cash, and then uses the proceeds to pay off as much of your unsecured debt as possible.

Chapter 7 works best for people who don't have a lot of assets, don't have steady income, and do have specific types of debts, such as:

- Medical debts
- Credit card debt
- Personal loans
- Personal lines of credit
- Overdue rent and utility bills

The whole process of Chapter 7 bankruptcy usually takes no more than six months from start to finish.

CHAPTER 13

If you just need more time, Chapter 13 gives it to you. Chapter 13 bankruptcy, also called reorganization bankruptcy, gives you the opportunity to pay off as much of your debt as possible over three to five years, sort of like a grace period. This allows you to catch up on debts—like your mortgage—that you've fallen behind on without having to sell off assets. Once your stay is granted, any attempts to foreclose on your house or repossess your car have to stop right away.

Chapter 13 works best for people who have:

- Reliable steady income
- Assets they want to keep
- Cosigners they'd like to protect

Any amount you still owe at the end of the Chapter 13 payoff period gets discharged.

HOW TO DECLARE BANKRUPTCY

While you can do it yourself, most people are better off working with an experienced bankruptcy attorney. If you forget a form or fill out the paperwork—and there's a lot of it—incorrectly, your case could be turned down or some of your debts may not be included. The steps may be a little different depending on where you live and which type of bankruptcy you file for, but the overall process will be similar.

To get started, you'll need to document a lot of information about your current financial situation—a lot of it similar to the information you've gathered while filling out the worksheets in this book. Before you file, you'll also have to complete some specific bankruptcy-related credit counseling. Make sure you get a certificate of completion, because your petition will get rejected without it.

Your attorney will help you get all of your paperwork in order and file your bankruptcy petition with the court. As soon as that's filed, most courts will grant the automatic stay to freeze all of the creditor actions. From there, a court-appointed trustee will take over your case and arrange a meeting with your creditors (and, yes, you have to be there in most cases). Depending on the type of bankruptcy, either you or the trustee will create a plan to deal with your creditors. Once that plan is approved and carried out, you'll need to take a debtor education course in order to complete the process.

Chapter Worksheets

The following worksheets will make it easier to manage your monthly cash flow. They'll help you prioritize and schedule your bills, identify painless ways to reduce expenses, and use credit cards and reward points strategically to benefit your budget. Downloadable Excel spreadsheets for each worksheet can be found at https://michelecagancpa .com/FinRec101 (with the password F1n@nc!@LRec0very!).

PRIORITIZE MONTHLY BILLS

✅ List your monthly bills in order of priority, starting with the most important. Pay attention to the point where your monthly income gets used up in this priority list. Be sure to make copies of this worksheet (at least three to six) before filling it out, as you'll need to fill out a copy for each month during your crisis and financial recovery. You can also find a downloadable version online at MicheleCaganCPA.com.

Notes:

MONTH:			
BILL DESCRIPTION	**PAYMENT DUE**	**DUE DATE**	**RUNNING TOTAL**
Total Monthly Bills			$

PAYING MONTHLY BILLS CALENDAR

✅ Use this calendar to map out which day each bill is due during the month. Include the name and amount due and check them off once paid. This will help you plan your cash flow, as you'll be able to see when money will be moving out. Be sure to make copies of this worksheet (about three to six) before filling it out, as you'll need to fill out a copy for each month during your crisis and financial recovery. You can also find a downloadable version online at MicheleCaganCPA.com.

MONTH:

SUNDAY	MONDAY	TUESDAY	WEDNESDAY	THURSDAY	FRIDAY	SATURDAY

HIDDEN EXPENSES CHECKLIST

✅ Use this checklist worksheet to find expenses that you may not realize you're paying. Uncovering these hidden expenses can help reduce your spending without causing any stress or cutbacks.

General

- ☐ Monthly bank account maintenance fee
- ☐ Paper statement fees (for banks or credit cards)
- ☐ Unused cell data
- ☐ Cell data overages
- ☐ Home phone/landline
- ☐ Credit card insurance
- ☐ In-app purchases
- ☐ Cable
- ☐ Investment fees
- ☐ Credit card annual fees

Unused Subscriptions

- ☐ Magazines
- ☐ Apps
- ☐ Streaming services
- ☐ Auto-ships
- ☐ Boxes (such as food or toiletries)
- ☐ Other

Unused Memberships

- ☐ Gym
- ☐ Club
- ☐ Retail
- ☐ Amazon Prime
- ☐ Other

Notes:

EXPENSES TO CUT

✓ To free up some space in your crisis budget, you'll need to cut some expenses. Some of these cuts will be temporary, and others may end up being permanent as you get used to them. Go through your checking account, credit card bills, and budgeting apps to find expenses you can ditch right away. Keep adding nonessential expenses to the following list until you free up as much cash flow as possible. Examples of these temporary cuts could include things like dog grooming, housekeeping, manicures, date nights, and restaurant meals.

TYPE OF EXPENSE	BUDGET CATEGORY	MONTHLY COST	CUMULATIVE FREED-UP BUDGET SPACE

SHOULD YOU CONSIDER BANKRUPTCY?

✅ Bankruptcy is a major life-changing decision, and it's not right for everyone. Answer the following questions by checking "Yes" or "No" to see whether it could be helpful for you.

QUESTION	YES	NO
Are you at least ninety days overdue on your debts?		
Will bankruptcy wipe out your most concerning debts?		
Are you getting contacted by collection agencies?		
Have your wages been garnished?		
Are you in danger of losing your home to foreclosure?		
Are you facing car repossession?		
Are you paying for essential expenses with credit cards?		
Do you make only minimum credit card payments?		
Have you pulled money from retirement accounts to pay bills?		
Will it take more than five years to pay off your credit card debt?		
Is your credit card debt greater than one year's salary?		
Have you tried to negotiate with creditors?		
Have you tried to refinance any of your debt?		

If you've answered yes to at least five of these questions, consider looking into your bankruptcy options.

WORKING WITH CREDITORS LOG

✅ As you contact your creditors, you'll want to keep detailed notes, especially if you contact them by phone. This checklist will help you make sure you record the most important information for each contact.

DATE AND TIME OF CONTACT	CREDITOR	TYPE OF CREDITOR	TOTAL AMOUNT DUE	CURRENT MONTHLY PAYMENT

Notes:

METHOD OF CONTACT	CONTACT INFO	CONTACT PERSON	NOTES AND DETAILS	FOL- LOW UP? Y/N

CREDIT CARD REWARDS DEALS

✓ Use this worksheet to help you get the most out of your credit card rewards points. Include upcoming bonus point deals and points "sales" for each card to help make the most of them.

REWARDS CARD	REWARD TYPE	AVAILABLE REWARDS	EXPIRATION DATE

Notes on Upcoming Deals:

USE FOR STATEMENT CREDITS?	GET CASH BACK?	GET GIFT CARDS?	POINTS USED	POINTS EARNED

CHAPTER SIX

GETTING BACK ON TRACK AND FORTIFYING YOUR FINANCES

Once you've come through your immediate financial crisis, you can start taking steps to restore your financial health and increase your financial security. In this middle zone between the financial crisis and full financial health, you'll be in true financial recovery. That calls for a recovery budget, one that sharply focuses on restoring savings and diminishing debt. This in-between budget keeps most of the cuts from the crisis budget and adds in higher levels of savings, debt paydown, or both...whatever makes the most sense for your specific financial situation.

In this chapter, you'll find everything you need to create your own recovery budget. At the same time, you'll continue paying close attention to how money flows into and out of your household and keep making mindful choices. This will help you identify any money leaks before they seriously drain your cash and uncover opportunities to increase your net worth without having to work harder. In this phase, you'll also work to rebuild your credit score, which will open up better, less expensive borrowing options for you in the future. Most important of all, you'll have more financial breathing room every month than you did during the worst of it, giving you the opportunity to set your finances on a more positive path. The steps you take now will create a foundation for building up your finances and creating lasting wealth. You've mastered the most important money habits as you've gone through this crisis, and now your financial health will improve at a much faster pace. And as your net worth continues to climb, you'll be locking in financial security for your family.

Create Your Recovery Budget

Your recovery budget may look very similar to your crisis budget, but it will feel much different. Since this budget kicks in once you're able to cover all of your essential expenses with income, rather than pulling from savings or adding to debt, it won't detract from your big financial picture. That's a huge accomplishment, and you should give yourself credit for getting here. In fact, every day you don't increase your debt or pull from savings—except in the case of a true emergency—counts as a win.

You'll still be living a leaner lifestyle during your recovery budget period, which acts like a bridge between your crisis finances and your future finances. But now, rather than just making ends meet, you'll be trying to create a sturdier financial foundation. That will include debt paydown and savings buildup as high priorities. Then you'll take that progress and use it as a platform to build solid, secure wealth for yourself and your family.

ADDING BACK EXPENSES

For now, your budget will still exclude most things that qualify as wants rather than needs, but it will give you a little more breathing room to spend carefully planned amounts on nonessentials. Check back in with the expenses you cut or reduced for your crisis budget. As more financial space becomes available, you'll be able to sort through those to figure out which you want to add back in, either now or when your finances are fully back on track. You may be surprised to find that there are a lot of things you used to spend money on that you just don't want to anymore.

Apply a mindful spending filter to each expense to help you decide if you even want to bring it back into your budget. Add back only expenses that serve you by making your life easier or better without causing budget overload. Any cost that you have been doing without that's gone unnoticed or hasn't caused any kind of distress or discomfort no longer deserves a spot in your budget. You can put that money to better use toward things that are more important to you. Add these return expenses back to your budget one at a time and in a way that matches your current financial goals.

GETTING BACK ON FINANCIAL TRACK

During this financial recovery period, you'll also take big steps to restore your finances to a precrisis state or beyond. You'll use your recovery budget as a tool to help you rebuild your savings and get control of your debt. This phase may last a while, depending on the depth of your financial crisis. But the strides you make toward financial recovery will be noticeable, and that momentum can help carry you through to the next part of your financial life: building wealth.

Pay Down Debt Before Building Savings

While you're still in financial recovery, you'll want to pay close attention to money flowing in and out. All money coming in that you don't need to use on essential expenses will go toward reestablishing security, and that means building savings and reducing debt. To do this successfully, you'll focus on one at a time, rather than devoting half measures to both.

If your crisis depleted your savings, your instincts may tell you to rebuild savings before tackling debt, but that can be a costly mistake. While it might feel less secure, it's much better for your overall financial health to focus on aggressively paying down debt—especially high-interest personal loans or credit card bills—before you turn to your savings goals. By taking this approach, you'll pay off debt much more quickly and save potentially thousands of dollars in interest, all of which can go toward funding robust savings.

CATCHING UP

If you paused or reduced bill and debt payments during the crisis, you'll want to catch up all of those accounts and get them to where they would have been. Depending on how your cash flow stacks up now, you can tackle one or more at a time, but it makes sense to catch up everything before you start moving anything forward. The exception: If you switched to a more manageable student loan repayment plan, you might want to keep that in place while you're taking more aggressive steps with other pieces of your financial puzzle.

Prioritize these catch-up payments in the way that makes the most sense for your financial situation. Generally speaking, this order works well for most people:

1. Mortgage or rent
2. Utility bills
3. Car loan
4. Student loans (in deferral or forbearance)
5. Credit cards
6. Other paused expenses or debts

Remember, we're not talking about full paydowns here. For now, you'll just be bringing these accounts current. That includes all missed payments or portions of payments plus any extra interest that has accrued during the payment time-out. Once everything is caught up, you can move on to the next phase of your financial recovery (detailed in the next section).

DOUBLING DOWN ON DEBT PAYOFF

When you want to get your debt paid off as quickly as possible, it pays to prioritize by interest rate, highest to lowest. For this paydown plan, you'll make minimum monthly payments on every debt, but you'll put any extra available cash toward your highest-rate debt. This will help reduce the total amount of interest you're paying, and speed up debt disappearance.

When less of your money has to go toward interest, more of it goes toward paying down the borrowed amount. As the principal portion of the debt decreases, so does the amount of interest charged, and the effect of that combination grows over time. As soon as your highest-rate debt gets paid off, you'll celebrate—or at the very least give yourself credit for this huge victory. Then you'll move its former payments to the next-highest-rate debt so you can tackle that one next. This payment strategy is known as the avalanche method, because of the quick, dramatic effect it has on your total outstanding debt.

> ### How Much Interest?
>
> To give you a sense of the huge bite high-rate interest takes out of debt payments, consider this: If you have a $5,000 balance on a credit card with an 18 percent interest rate, the first $75 of your payment goes straight toward interest. You can see why trying to pay off high-rate debt feels like an uphill battle…and why paying it off first and fast will free up the most possible cash for you.

There are other debt paydown strategies out there, but this method will help free you of debt most quickly and with the least damage to your overall finances. However, if you do better with a different type of plan, such as one where you pay off individual debts more quickly regardless of interest rate, use the plan that will keep you motivated.

Use the Accelerated Debt Repayment worksheet at the end of this chapter to set up your aggressive debt payoff plan. Mark your progress periodically—but not too often—to give yourself the satisfaction of watching your debt level drop dramatically.

Shore Up Your Savings

Once you're ready to start building up savings, you'll want to split your resources between retirement and emergency accounts. Think about it this way: Your retirement accounts are your *future* emergency and regular savings, the money you'll have available to cover your expenses after you've stopped working full-time. So you'll want to build up both your current and future emergency savings at the same time.

The following is what your aggressive super-saving campaign will look like.

STEP 1: CONTRIBUTE AS MUCH AS YOU CAN TO RETIREMENT SAVINGS

If you have an employer-sponsored account, such as a 401(k) or 403(b), contribute at least enough to trigger employer matching (if that's available). If you don't have access to an employer-sponsored retirement plan, contribute what you can to an IRA (individual retirement account).

This step is especially important if you had to pull money out of your retirement accounts to get through your financial crisis. If you borrowed money from a 401(k), you may not be able to make current contributions until that loan is paid back in full. So do that first, and then get back to a regular retirement funding schedule.

Know Your Limits

Maximum contribution limits change annually for all types of retirement accounts: employer-based, self-employed, and individual. The IRS imposes penalties for excess contributions, so make sure you know your limits, especially when they're not for employer-based plans. You can find out the contribution limit for your type of plan for the current year by visiting the IRS website at www.irs.gov.

Use the Retirement Savings Needs worksheet at the end of this chapter to figure out how much money you'll need to support the retirement you want, along with the monthly contributions that will get you there.

STEP 2: REPLENISH YOUR EMERGENCY SAVINGS

If you don't already have a separate, dedicated emergency savings account, create one. It's best to keep this money at least one step removed from your checking account, so you're not tempted to dip into it for paying regular bills. Your best choice: an FDIC-insured high-interest (and "high" is a relative term here) online savings account. These accounts limit the number of withdrawals you can make each month, so you'll have to plan those out carefully when you do need to use your emergency funds.

Use the Build Up Emergency Savings worksheet at the end of this chapter to figure out how much money you need in your emergency fund and how much you need to save periodically to reach that savings goal.

For Emergencies Only

Avoid using your emergency savings for anything that's not actually an emergency. Many people dip into these accounts for things like semiannual insurance payments and car maintenance costs. Sometimes these funds get used to keep budgets in balance. But the point of an emergency fund is to handle unexpected spending situations. So before you dip into this account, consider if the reason for the dip is actually an emergency. For example, a $500 scheduled car maintenance service is *not* an emergency, but $200 to replace a blown tire is.

To handle periodic spending situations, like insurance and oil changes, add them as monthly line items in your budget. You can do that by converting the periodic expense into a monthly expense. Then put the full monthly amount into a "periodic expenses savings account" (or whatever you want to call it) so the money will be there when you're ready for it.

Keep Tracking Your Finances Regularly

The best way to take charge of your financial situation involves keeping tabs on it. You may not need to check in as often as you did during the crisis, but you'll want to track your cash flow regularly, *at least* once a month. By doing that, you'll be able to catch and correct potential problems before they grow into bigger issues that can damage your financial situation.

PLANNING AHEAD FOR MAJOR SPENDING

Spend-ahead plans might seem like they're the same as goals, but they're not. Goals involve things you want to do, and center around your lifestyle. Spend-ahead plans help you "prepay" for big purchases that you know are coming up. For example, if you know your hot water heater only has about a year or two left, you can start a separate water heater savings account that will allow you to pay cash for the appliance and related labor.

Take It from a CPA

During a lean period, my dishwasher started leaking. It still worked to get the dishes clean, but we'd end up with a puddle on the floor every time we ran it. So I started a "new dishwasher fund" to help me replace it, rather than just buy a new appliance on credit. And in the meantime, we just put a Tupperware container where the leak was. Clean dishes, no puddle, and time to save up for a new dishwasher.

It's sort of the opposite of putting the new water heater on a credit card or plumber's payment plan. Instead of buying the water heater and then paying for it monthly, usually plus interest, you do the reverse. You save money every month toward that purchase and *earn* interest on your "prepayments." This type of spend-ahead planning works for all major purchases except for emergencies, which would be covered by your emergency savings. You'll use this strategy for any large expenditure you can possibly predict, from a kitchen remodel to a new TV to an upcoming major car repair. Include these spend-ahead plans as line items in your budget to make sure you set aside the money you need.

USE A BUDGETING APP FOR NO-HASSLE TRACKING

As you take control of your finances and gain new insights, you eventually might want to switch from worksheets to a more automatic system for managing your money. Budgeting apps take all the busywork out of tracking your income and expenses while providing you with valuable information and tools to manage your cash flow.

Not Comfortable Connecting Accounts?

If having all of your financial information connected in one app makes you uncomfortable, you can go lower tech and work with manual budgeting spreadsheets instead. These will be more labor-intensive, but they'll also keep you more intimately connected with your cash flow. Most spreadsheet programs include preset budget templates to help you get started. And most bank and investment accounts let you download statements in .csv format that you can easily import into your spreadsheet (so you don't have to type stuff in).

No matter which budgeting app you choose to use—and there are a lot of them—the setup will be your biggest time commitment. It takes time to connect your accounts, teach the app how you want transactions to be categorized, and get used to all the features. But once that's all done, you'll be able to check in on your budget any time, any day, and as often as you like. You can try out a few different apps to see which feels most comfortable and intuitive for you, and which works best for your financial and family situation.

Favorite apps among my clients include:

- **PocketGuard:** a budgeting app that's designed to prevent over-spending in any budget category, and actively looks for ways that you can save on regular monthly bills (like phone and Internet).
- **Mint:** a good full-service budgeting app that combines big-picture and detailed financial tracking.
- **Mvelopes:** a cash-style budgeting app that keeps virtual "envelopes" of cash (including credit and debit card spending) for each budget category, and lets you know when each envelope has been fully spent for the month.
- **Goodbudget:** an envelope system designed for couples (though it works for singles also) who want to sync up their shared finances.
- **YNAB (You Need a Budget):** a zero-based income-focused budgeting app that assigns a role to every dollar before it's spent, and has special tracking features for things like debt pay-down and goal progress.

If you want to use an automated spreadsheet program instead of an app, look into Tiller Money. With direct connections to your accounts—just like an app—Tiller Money offers real-time financial tracking in spreadsheet format. The program is flexible and lets you customize spreadsheets to fit your unique situation and needs. You can set up unlimited budget categories and set up budgets for custom time periods (by the week or biweekly, rather than just monthly, for example).

MORE THAN TRACKING YOUR BUDGET

Financial tracking involves more than keeping tabs on your budget, though that's a great first step. In addition to your monthly income and expenses, you'll also want to pay attention to progress and changes in your:

- Net worth
- Retirement accounts
- Non-retirement investment accounts
- Debt profile
- Credit score

You can track any of these manually or through apps, and some apps offer you the ability to track several (possibly even all) of these aspects of your financial life at once. The two most comprehensive money management apps are:

1. **Personal Capital:** tracks net worth, savings, budget, debt paydown, retirement, and non-retirement investments.
2. **Mint:** tracks budget, net worth, credit score, debt, and investments.

Each of these aspects factor into your overall financial picture, contributing a critical piece of the puzzle.

Know Your Debt Profile

Your debt profile is more about the character of your debt than the amount (though that does play a role). To gain financial security, you'll want to shift your debt from wealth crushing to wealth producing. Wealth-crushing debt includes personal loans and credit cards, debt that costs a lot in interest but does nothing to further your finances. Wealth-producing debt includes things like mortgages, small business loans, and student loans—borrowing that increases your wealth *potential* and typically comes with much lower interest rates.

Tracking any one of these factors on its own will show you in-depth information about that piece, while tracking all of them together gives you the big-picture view of your financial situation. When you can see the whole puzzle at once, you can make better choices to further your financial security and independence.

Build Up Your Financial Security and Net Worth

Financial security means *never* being afraid you're going to lose your house, get your lights shut off, have your car repossessed. It means not having to stay at a job you hate, or constantly worrying about having your hours cut back or getting fired, laid off, or downsized. It means *knowing* that even if you face another financial emergency, you'll be able to make it through.

True financial security comes from a place of strong net worth and diverse income sources. When you have unrelated resources to draw from, a drop in any one of them won't send you into a catastrophic financial spiral. Having more options equals more security, and this is the perfect time to continue branching out.

Coming off of a financial setback is the best time to make a plan to build up your net worth, the pool of financial resources you'll have available to you moving forward. Over time, you want your net worth to grow steadily, which will stabilize your financial security. No matter what it looks like now, even if it's negative, you can develop a strategy to increase your net worth.

BUILDING YOUR NET WORTH

You can dramatically increase your net worth by taking a two-pronged approach: acquiring income-producing assets and reducing unproductive debt. Either of these directions will take you closer to financial security and independence. You can do both at the same time, but it's generally better to completely rid yourself of unproductive and high-interest-rate debt before adding assets to your nest egg.

In most cases, decreasing debt—especially debt that costs more than your money could reasonably earn—comes first.

Unproductive debt (debt that costs a lot of money but offers you nothing in exchange) usually stems from high-interest credit card debt, personal loans, and toxic debts such as payday loans. It's typically used to pay for expenses rather than acquire assets. Paying down this debt offers guaranteed returns: You will absolutely not have to pay more interest on debt that has been paid. So if, for example, you pay off credit card debt that came with 18 percent APR (annual percentage rate), you used your money to earn back that 18 percent. No savings account and very few investments will earn you that kind of return, so paying it off gave your net worth the biggest possible boost.

That doesn't mean you'll need to stop borrowing money altogether, though. Productive debt gives you the opportunity to purchase assets—like investments or businesses—that will create more income than the interest on the related debt. Strategically using low-rate debt to buy income-producing assets gives you more opportunities to grow your net worth and develop true wealth.

That's the flip side of net worth building that depends on asset growth: putting your assets to work earning money for you. When successful, these assets can supply steady cash flow and grow your net worth without you having to devote a lot of time and effort to it. Income-producing assets include things like:

- Stocks
- Bonds
- Mutual funds
- Real estate
- Small business

And these types of assets will generate your next layer of financial security: income streams (more on this in the next section).

> ### The Time Factor
>
> The longer your assets have to earn money for you, the more they'll grow on their own. That means you'll want to start accumulating productive assets as early as possible, so you can take advantage of more time. It's important, though, to fully understand the pros, cons, and potential of every asset you consider adding to your nest egg. None of them will make you an overnight fortune, so you want to look for high-quality bargains—and that takes time, effort, and research.

Learn as much as you can about any asset you plan to purchase, whether it's a rental property or a mutual fund. You're buying these assets for the long haul, to build a foundation of wealth and cash flow for years—maybe generations—to come.

FINANCIAL SECURITY THROUGH DIVERSE INCOME STREAMS

When you have multiple ways to bring in money, you won't be wholly dependent on any one of them. Any income stream—especially those you have less control over—could dry up suddenly due to a job loss, stock market crash, disaster-stricken rental property, or other unexpected situation. Setting up as many income sources as you can dilutes the potential negative impact of each one. If one disappears—even if it's the most lucrative one—you still have income from other sources coming in.

Having multiple income streams gives you the opportunity to walk away from a job that's not right for you (for any reason), to risk asking for things like a raise or additional paid time off (or even unpaid, for that matter), or to sell an investment that no longer fits into your plans no matter what the market's doing. And on the other side, having multiple income streams in place can make it easier to do things like buy a house or launch a passion project.

Of course, these cash flows don't pop up overnight. Rather, it can take time to set them up and even more time before they're providing predictable cash. So, the sooner you get started, the sooner you'll have an additional source of reliable income.

Active income streams, meaning ones that involve ongoing engagement on your part, include:

- Writing and selling an ebook or online course
- Taking paid surveys with companies like Survey Junkie and Swagbucks
- Long-term side gigs, where you build up a steady client base
- App-based side gigs, where you work only when you want to, such as Rover, Instacart, or TaskRabbit
- Creating apps or products to sell

But while side gigs and second jobs do provide new sources of income, they also require continued commitments of time and effort. Since you have a fixed amount of available time, you can't have unlimited income streams that rely on you working. That's why you need to have some passive income streams as well.

Passive income streams, meaning cash sources that don't require any current effort on your part, can be extremely helpful here. They supply income without taking up your time once they're set up—literally letting you earn money while you sleep. Putting in the effort to create and stabilize passive income streams will substantially increase your financial freedom, flexibility, and security. Some take a hefty cash outlay to set up; others can be started with less than $50, and still others cost no money—just time. Some will start slow and gradually build up, while others will just add a little cash boost when you need it. Start wherever you're comfortable and keep adding distinct income streams into your mix.

The Tax Cost of Passive Income

Just like income you get from a job, passive income is taxable. But because of the way the US tax system works, passive income is often taxed at lower rates than the income you earn through employment. Plus, passive income is *not* subject to "payroll taxes," Social Security, or Medicare, which eat up 7.65 percent of your paycheck, or 15.3 percent of your self-employment income.

Commonly used passive income streams include things like:

- Ad revenues from a website or channel (like a *YouTube* channel)
- Affiliate marketing, where you earn commissions when people click on specific links on a website you own or through your social media
- Royalties from a work (like a book or piece of music) you created
- Interest on high-yield savings accounts, money market accounts, or laddered CDs (certificates of deposit)
- Income from investments such as dividend stocks and REITs (real estate investment trusts)
- Rents from properties you own (either wholly or partially)
- Profits from an ongoing business that doesn't require your constant attention

The more opportunities you have to bring in money, the more quickly you'll be able to reach your financial goals...and start working toward new ones.

REVISITING AND REVISING YOUR FINANCIAL GOALS

Once you're on the other side of your financial emergency, you'll be ready to transform your crisis goals into recovery goals and set new forward-looking goals. These goals will help create the framework for the rest of your financial planning. For example, a recovery goal of paying off all non-mortgage debt within three years calls for different money moves than one to replenish $40,000 to retirement savings within five years.

Then comes the really fun part: dream-life goals. Think about what you want to do with your life. Each of these can be turned into a goal. And once you have a clear goal, you can create a plan to reach it. To that end, you want to make sure your goals are SMART.

SMART goals are:

- **S**pecific
- **M**easurable
- **A**chievable
- **R**ealistic
- **T**ime-bound

So rather than saying you want to buy a dream house, you'll craft a SMART goal. For example, "I want to buy a $300,000 house with a big backyard in the Richmond area in five years with a 20 percent down payment and a low-rate mortgage."

That goal is *specific*, rich with details. It's *measurable* because it builds in the down payment savings subgoal. Saving $60,000 over five years ($1,000 per month) and maintaining an excellent credit score will make this goal *achievable*. It's *realistic* if the income, incoming cash flow, and budgeting needs allow for that additional savings. And the five-year part of the plan gives it a clear *time boundary*. It works the same way for financial recovery goals too: The more detailed you make them, the easier it will be to lay out a plan to achieve them.

DEALING WITH SETBACKS QUICKLY

Financial setbacks can come from anywhere—a sudden medical issue, a stock market decline, or an employer going bankrupt, just to name a few. And, truthfully, there will almost always be a next crisis to deal with, because that's just the way life works. But when you have control over and a clear view of your full financial picture, these setbacks will seem more like blips than crises.

Not only will you have the resources in place to deal with anything that crops up; you'll also have the skills you've learned here to apply to the next situation. You'll be able to identify problem areas before they erupt into full-scale catastrophes. You'll know exactly what steps to take to begin damage control and will be able to implement those moves at top speed. The sooner you contain the problem, the faster your finances will rebound. Then you can focus on creating additional layers of security for proactive protection against whatever comes next.

Chapter Worksheets

The following worksheets will move you through financial recovery with an eye on the future. You'll take clear steps to improve your credit score, a key component of ongoing financial health. You'll transform your budget from survival mode to recovery mode, and begin slowly adding back some "want" expenses you were forced to cut during the crisis. By completing these worksheets, you'll be taking the first steps into a financially secure future. Downloadable Excel spreadsheets for each worksheet can be found at https://michelecagancpa.com/FinRec101 (with the password F1n@nc!@LRec0very!).

RESTORING YOUR CREDIT SCORE

✅ Follow the steps of the following checklist to increase your credit score, recording your score in the provided table now, in ninety days, in six months, and in twelve months in order to track changes. It won't happen overnight, but you should start seeing positive results within three months. Once your score hits good territory, keep it there by tracking your utilization every month and reviewing your full credit report every year.

DATE	CURRENT CREDIT SCORE
NINETY-DAY CHECKBACK DATE	**UPDATED CREDIT SCORE**
SIX-MONTH CHECKBACK DATE	**UPDATED CREDIT SCORE**
TWELVE-MONTH CHECKBACK DATE	**UPDATED CREDIT SCORE**

Check off each step as you complete it:

Part One: Make Corrections to Your Credit Report

- ☐ Review your credit report for accuracy
- ☐ Note any errors on the report
- ☐ Gather documentation to dispute each error
- ☐ Report each error to the appropriate credit bureau

Part Two: Be a Bill-Paying Star

- ☐ Pay every bill on time every month
- ☐ Pay down outstanding credit card balances
- ☐ Get credit for utility, phone, and rent payments

Part Three: Control Your Credit

- ☐ Don't apply for any new loans or credit cards
- ☐ Don't cancel any credit cards, even ones you've paid off
- ☐ Use the table provided to track your utilization and keep it as low as possible

TRACK UTILIZATION	
MONTH	**UTILIZATION %**
1	
2	
3	
4	
5	
6	
7	
8	
9	
10	
11	
12	

RECOVERY BUDGET

✓ This budget serves as a bridge between your crisis budget and your regular budget. Once essential expenses are met, all additional income goes toward reducing debt and rebuilding savings.

MONTH:	
TOTAL EXPECTED INCOME	$
EXPENSE	**$ AMOUNT**
Rent or mortgage payment	
Food	
Childcare	
Utilities:	
Gas and electric	
Phone	
Water	
Internet	
Transportation:	
License and registration	
Gas	
Scheduled maintenance	
Healthcare:	
Scheduled doctor visits	
Medicine	
Scheduled dental	
Insurance:	
Health	
Auto	

Homeowners or renters	
Life	
Other	
Minimum debt payments	
Necessary clothing	
Other expense	
Other expense	
Other expense	
Total expenses	$
Money left after necessary expenses*	$
Additional debt paydown	
Retirement savings (if not a paycheck deduction)	
Emergency savings	

*Use all of the remaining money to pay down debt or build savings until your budget zeroes out.

Notes:

BUILD UP EMERGENCY SAVINGS

✓ In this worksheet, you'll start right-sizing your emergency savings by figuring out how much cash you need to have stockpiled in order to feel financially secure. Once you've set that goal, you'll begin contributing toward it and tracking your progress every month. Don't worry if you have to pull money out to cover an emergency—that's what this fund is for. Expect the balance to go up and down, and work to replenish the account whenever necessary.

Step 1: Set Your Emergency Savings Goal

ESSENTIAL MONTHLY EXPENSES			
ONE MONTH	**THREE MONTHS**	**SIX MONTHS**	**TWELVE MONTHS**
Average Total Monthly Expenses*		$	

*If your household has a single income stream, use one of the twelve-month values for your emergency savings goal. If there are multiple reliable income streams in place, set one of the three- or six-month values for your goal.

Notes:

Step 2: Track Your Emergency Savings Progress*

EMERGENCY SAVINGS GOAL		
MONTH	**ENDING BALANCE**	**NEED TO SAVE**
1		
2		
3		
4		
5		
6		
7		
8		
9		
10		
11		
12		

*While this table has room to track for twelve months, you'll want to make copies (or use the downloadable worksheet found online at MicheleCaganCPA.com) and track indefinitely, as the balance will inevitably go up and down over time.

Notes:

RETIREMENT SAVINGS NEEDS

✅ This worksheet will give you a very general idea of your retirement budget needs and the amount of money you'll need to save monthly to reach them. It does not take into account taxes, investment choices, expected rate of return, or compounding—all of which could change the amount you need to save. Updating this worksheet at least annually will give you a clearer picture of how close you are to achieving your goal.

HOW MUCH DO YOU NEED TO RETIRE?*	
GUARANTEED MONTHLY INCOME EXPECTED (SOURCE)	**$ AMOUNT FROM SOURCE**
Pension	
Annuity	
Social Security	
Total Guaranteed Income	
TOTAL MONTHLY RETIREMENT EXPENSES	$
ADDITIONAL AMOUNT NEEDED FROM SAVINGS EACH MONTH**	$
ANNUAL AMOUNT NEEDED FROM SAVINGS***	$

*Use this section to get a basic idea of the total amount you'll need to have saved before you retire.
**Subtract guaranteed income from monthly expenses to see how much more you'll need each month.
***Multiply additional amount needed each month by twelve.

Notes:

TOTAL RETIREMENT SAVINGS TARGET*	
YEARS IN RETIREMENT	**SAVINGS NEEDED**
20	
30	
40	
Your Retirement Savings Total**	$

*For a retirement lasting X years, you'll need this much money. Multiply the number of years by the annual amount needed from savings for the total retirement goal.
**Use the goal that best fits your time frame or an average of the three calculated goals.

HOW MUCH DO YOU HAVE SAVED FOR RETIREMENT?*			
ACCOUNT NAME	**TYPE**	**BALANCE**	**AS OF DATE**
TOTAL CURRENT RETIREMENT SAVINGS		$	

*List the current value of all retirement accounts here.

MONEY IN, MONEY OUT

✅ This worksheet takes a different look at your budget, focusing on all money in and out for the previous month. Money in will include only cash brought in that's available for spending, such as your paycheck, 1099 income, or investment income. Money out includes all forms of spending, like credit cards, credit card points, and other noncash spending. This acts as a double check on your budget to help make sure that money out does not exceed money in, or to let you know as soon as possible if it does. You'll want to make copies of this worksheet in order to complete it for a solid nine months. A downloadable version of this worksheet can also be found online at MicheleCaganCPA.com.

MONTH:	
MONEY IN	**$ AMOUNT**
Paycheck	
Side gig/1099	
Investment income	
Other	
Total Money In	$
MONEY OUT	**$ AMOUNT**
Total cash spent to pay bills	
ATM withdrawals and fees	
Other banking fees	
Credit card spending	
Rewards points used (in $)	
Other noncash spending	
Total Money Out	$
MONEY IN – MONEY OUT*	$

*If money in minus money out is negative, that means total spending exceeded total income for that month.

ACCELERATED DEBT REPAYMENT

✓ List all of your debts in order of interest rate, from highest to lowest. Make minimum payments on all debts. The outstanding debt with the highest rate will be your first focus debt. All available cash from the budget will go toward making an extra payment on the focus debt. When a debt gets paid off, you can add its payments to your new focus debt.

	FOCUS DEBT ORDER				
DEBT NUMBER	**DEBT NAME**	**INTEREST RATE**	**OUT-STANDING BALANCE**	**MINIMUM PAYMENT**	**PAYMENT DUE DATE**
1					
2					
3					
4					
5					
6					
7					
8					
9					
10					
Totals			$	$	

DEBT PAYDOWN TABLE

✅ Get the monthly balance from your statements every month so you don't have to figure out what portion of your payment went toward principal and so you can take into account any new charges. This section of the worksheet will help you track balances and let you know when it's time to switch to the next focus debt. You will want to make copies of this worksheet in order to continue filling it out until you are down to one or no debts. You can also find a downloadable version online at MicheleCaganCPA.com.

Notes:

MONTH	TOTAL $ AVAILABLE FOR DEBT PAYDOWN	TOTAL MINIMUM PAYMENT	EXTRA PAYMENT FOR FOCUS DEBT
1			
2			
3			
4			
5			
6			
7			
8			
9			
10			
11			
12			
13			
14			
15			
16			
17			
18			
19			
20			
21			
22			
23			
24			

OUTSTANDING DEBT BALANCE AT THE *BEGINNING* OF THIS

MONTH	DEBT 1	DEBT 2	DEBT 3	DEBT 4
1	$	$	$	$
2	$	$	$	$
3	$	$	$	$
4	$	$	$	$
5	$	$	$	$
6	$	$	$	$
7	$	$	$	$
8	$	$	$	$
9	$	$	$	$
10	$	$	$	$
11	$	$	$	$
12	$	$	$	$
13	$	$	$	$
14	$	$	$	$
15	$	$	$	$
16	$	$	$	$
17	$	$	$	$
18	$	$	$	$
19	$	$	$	$
20	$	$	$	$
21	$	$	$	$
22	$	$	$	$
23	$	$	$	$
24	$	$	$	$

DEBT 5	DEBT 6	DEBT 7	DEBT 8	DEBT 9	DEBT 10
$	$	$	$	$	$
$	$	$	$	$	$
$	$	$	$	$	$
$	$	$	$	$	$
$	$	$	$	$	$
$	$	$	$	$	$
$	$	$	$	$	$
$	$	$	$	$	$
$	$	$	$	$	$
$	$	$	$	$	$
$	$	$	$	$	$
$	$	$	$	$	$
$	$	$	$	$	$
$	$	$	$	$	$
$	$	$	$	$	$
$	$	$	$	$	$
$	$	$	$	$	$
$	$	$	$	$	$
$	$	$	$	$	$
$	$	$	$	$	$
$	$	$	$	$	$
$	$	$	$	$	$
$	$	$	$	$	$
$	$	$	$	$	$

NEW AND REVISED GOALS

✓ Use this template to create your moving-forward financial goals. Use the SMART goal strategy when creating your goals. You can add the monthly amount to your budget based on your start date. Keep your goals flexible and make adjustments as needed.

GOAL	TOTAL $ NEEDED
Financial Goal #1:	
Financial Goal #2:	
Financial Goal #3:	
Financial Goal #4:	
Financial Goal #5:	

Notes:

TIME FRAME	TIME FRAME (IN MONTHS)	MONTHLY $ NEEDED	EXPECTED START DATE	EXPECTED END DATE

CONCLUSION

TAKING STOCK AND MOVING FORWARD

Congratulations! You've made it this far, which means you're working through this book and taking charge of your financial situation. As frustrating, frightening, and just plain hard as your financial crisis is and has been, you're doing everything you can to move through it—and come out financially stronger on the other side.

You have a more in-depth understanding of your finances. You know which moves to make to keep your budget from boiling over during financial setbacks. And you know how to build up your resources for a stronger level of financial security. But this is not where you'll stop. You'll keep moving your finances forward, increasing your net worth and expanding your income streams, and creating lasting wealth for yourself and your family.

You Are Not Alone

One of the most important things to remember here is that you are not alone. Financial struggles can make you feel alone and isolated, and like *everything* falls on you. But it doesn't. There's a lot of help available, in many different forms, and you can take advantage of whatever kind of help works for you.

Clients of mine have gone through a range of difficult financial situations, and some have called on me for help right away, while others reached out as a last resort. Either way, they've talked about feeling an overwhelming sense of relief when they had someone else to help manage the burden—even just small parts of it. Don't wait until you're feeling burned out or like you're drowning to ask for help. The time to get help is right away, because every little bit of assistance will make it that much easier to move through your financial crisis.

You Have the Skills

You can also rely on the skills you've gained while working through this book. These skills were designed to help you create and strengthen financial confidence and security. Through the guidance and worksheets in this book, you've taken concrete steps toward:

- Setting clear, achievable goals
- Increasing your net worth
- Creating and maintaining multiple income streams
- Planning ahead for major spending
- Tracking your finances regularly
- Dealing with setbacks quickly

Keep exercising these skills to propel your finances forward, create financial stability, and be better able to weather—or even prevent—the next financial snag that crops up.

That's the silver lining here: how much stronger your money management powers have grown. You've established an amazing foundation to build on. With a complete sense of your current financial situation, you know which areas can use more attention, whether that's learning more about investing, improving debt management, or creating substantial passive income streams. And the more you learn, the better you'll be able to improve your current and future finances. So, now, you'll want to build on your financial knowledge. The following Resources section is a great place to start.

RESOURCES

There are (probably) millions of free personal financial resources available online, but they're not all accurate or reliable. Anyone can start a personal finance blog, write a book, or create a course, whether or not they have any credentials or experience. So you'll want to do a little checking before you rely on what a complete stranger tells you about how to handle your money. Begin with this list to discover the many opportunities to help your finances flourish.

BOOKS

- *The Automatic Millionaire* by David Bach
- *Choose Your Retirement* by Emily Guy Birken
- *The Intelligent Investor* by Benjamin Graham
- *The Bogleheads' Guide to Investing* by Taylor Larimore
- *Broke Millennial Takes On Investing* by Erin Lowry
- *The Mindful Millionaire* by Leisa Peterson
- *Your Money or Your Life* by Vicki Robin
- *I Will Teach You to Be Rich* by Ramit Sethi
- *The 21-Day Financial Fast* by Michelle Singletary
- *Grow Your Money* by Bola Sokunbi

PODCASTS

- *Stacking Benjamins*
- *Mental Health and Wealth*
- *Money Circle*
- *CentsAble Chat*
- *So Money*
- *Planet Money*
- *BiggerPockets*
- *Afford Anything*
- *His & Her Money*
- *Money for the Rest of Us*
- *Michelle Is Money Hungry*
- *Taxgirl*
- *Yo Quiero Dinero*

WEBSITES FOR INFORMATION RESOURCES

National Consumer Law Center (NCLC)
www.nclc.org

Federal Trade Commission
www.ftc.gov

Consumer Financial Protection Bureau (CFPB)
www.consumerfinance.gov

IRS (Internal Revenue Service)
www.irs.gov

Let's Make a Plan
www.letsmakeaplan.org

360 Degrees of Financial Literacy
www.360financialliteracy.org

FINRA for Investors
www.finra.org/investors#/

SEC (US Securities and Exchange Commission)
www.sec.gov

Michele Cagan, CPA
https://michelecagancpa.com/
FinRec101
password: F1n@nc!@LRec0very!

BLOGS

The Balance
www.thebalance.com

Financial IQ by Susie Q
https://financialiqbysusieq.com

Brave Saver
https://bravesaver.com

NerdWallet
www.nerdwallet.com

Investopedia
www.investopedia.com

Saving Joyfully
https://savingjoyfully.com

A Dime Saved
https://adimesaved.com

Jean Chatzky
www.jeanchatzky.com

Debt Free Guys
https://debtfreeguys.com

The Fioneers
https://thefioneers.com

Budgets Are Sexy
www.budgetsaresexy.com

Making Sense of Cents
www.makingsenseofcents.com

INDEX

ABOUT THE AUTHOR

Michele Cagan is a CPA, author, and financial mentor. With more than twenty years of experience, she offers unique insights into personal financial planning, from breaking out of debt and minimizing taxes, to maximizing income and building wealth. Michele has written numerous articles and books about personal finance, investing, and accounting, including *The Infographic Guide to Personal Finance, Debt 101, Investing 101,* and *Retirement 101.* In addition to her financial know-how, Michele has a not-so-secret love of painting, Star Wars, and chocolate. She lives in Maryland with her son, dogs, cats, and koi. Get more financial guidance from Michele by visiting MicheleCaganCPA.com.